Memories

of an

East End Child

Autobiographical Stories

Violet Harrington

Memories of an East End Child
Autobiographical Stories
©2024 Violet Harrington

Published by Texianer Verlag
Tuningen
Germany

www.texianer.com

ISBN: 978-3-910667-09-9

All rights reserved

Contents

THE AUTHOR	5
Memories of an East End Child *Violet Harrington*	7
My Mum! *Lorraine Harrington*	45
My Dad *Violet Harrington*	59
Choices! *Lorraine Roxon*	73
A Golden Oldie in Cyber Space. *Lorraine Roxon*	91
My Grandson Gabriel 1973-1991 *Lorraine Roxon*	109
We Are What We Are *Lorraine Harrington*	117
For Jean *2nd March 2009*	127
Jennifer's Ride *Lorraine Roxon* *Jennifer and David September 2nd 2006*	129

THE AUTHOR

I was born on the 12th of February 1927 and named Violet Eunice Smith. I became a Lucy Clayton fashion model in 1947 and it was suggested that I use the name Lorraine. So while modelling I was known as Lorraine Smith.

In 1949 I married Dr David Ropschitz and so became Violet Eunice Ropschitz. I divorced David in 1974 and five years later while on holiday in New Zealand I met Cyril Harrington. I went to New Zealand to live with Cyril where we opened the first sun tanning clinic in the country.

I decided that Violet Ropschitz was not a suitable business name, so I became Lorraine Roxon. Roxon was the name used by several family members and my three children used the name Roxon at school. Lillian Roxon is well known for her journalistic career in America and wrote 'The Encyclopaedia of Rock'.

My youngest son Gordon, legally became Gordon Roxon and my eldest son, Manfred Roxon became an investigative journalist. So, with the name Lorraine from my modelling career and Roxon I became known in business and the art world as Lorraine Roxon. This proved to be successful and later I became the director of the Lorraine Roxon Beauty School.

In 1993 Cy and I married, and I became Violet Harrington. I still use the name Lorraine Roxon for my paintings, sculpture and writing. I am mostly known now as Lorraine except by my family who still call me Violet.

Memories of an East End Child

Violet Harrington

Illustration 1: Photo taken 1933. Left to right. Donald, Violet and Harry.

The Isle of Dogs is an area in the East End of London. Some say it was given that name because Queen Elizabeth I ran her dogs on the island when she was in residence at Greenwich Palace. Others say its present name is a corruption of the 'Isle of Docks' over the centuries, but no one really knows for certain. I like to think of Queen Elizabeth with her courtiers, crossing the Thames in their royal barges and letting the dogs run. It certainly conjures up a more interesting picture. It is called an island because the area is surrounded by water and it is situated in the 'U' of the River Thames. To leave the island, you had to cross a bridge or go under the river by a foot tunnel.

When World War II was declared I was twelve-and-a-half years of age. I had previously attended Cubitt Town Infants School but had passed my exams and was now at Millwall Central Grammar School. My name was Violet Smith and we were a family of six. There was Mum, Dad and my three younger brothers. I remember us as a close, loving family. I believe the war did a lot of harm, but as the saying goes, "Out of evil cometh good", and the one good that came out of the bombing was the demolition of houses ridden with bugs, mice and fleas. Most of these slum houses were owned by the church, and I can understand why my parents were non-believers and could see no good in religion when church authorities allowed such houses to exist, whilst collecting rent from poor people. But our house was not one of them, and Dad, being a master-builder and decorator, kept it in good order.

The area is now very different and part of it is called the Docklands. New, expensive town houses have been built where the wharves once were, and by their sides are moorings for their owners' boats. I have even heard it called a yuppie area.

As a child, I would sit in Island Gardens, a park at the end of our street. The gardens had a playground with a cafeteria and the river Thames flowed past. This is where the underground tunnel to Greenwich is situated. It stands as it was, unchanged by the war. Before the war it was usual for me to sit on one of the park benches on my own and watch the boats go up and down the river laden with cargo. The Thames was always dark brown and murky with bits of old wood and rubbish floating along in the current. Hours would go by and I would write down the names and draw the flags of the boats as they sailed along the river.

Because I was a child with a lively imagination quite a lot of my time was spent daydreaming. My thoughts would carry me away to the countries the boats had come from. Here there was a particular smell, which can still easily evoke memories of the past. When a mist surrounded the area, the smell became more prominent. Of the many things that made up the smell was something called locust. There would be lots of it lying on the ground in the street near the wharves and we children would pick it up and eat it. It was sweet to taste and many years later while on holiday in Spain I saw this curved fruit hanging from the tree. In Spain, the fruit was a nice, fresh, green colour, but it was black and dried when we used to eat it. We had no idea whether it was suitable for human consumption, but we all ate it and no harm came to us. I think it was ground down and used as cattle feed. In those days, children never thought of hygiene and maybe a few of the germs we picked up gave us some protection from disease.

Lots of children would go to the wharves and play on the barges moored by the river, but my brothers and I were never allowed to go near them because Mum and Dad told us it was dangerous and that children had been known to drown or be crushed between two barges. We never heard of any child getting hurt, but that was the story Mum and Dad told us and it was good enough to keep us away. I did go with a friend a couple of times and was amazed at the pieces of broken white clay pipe that were washed up on the muddy beach. I would take a few pieces and use them to draw hopscotch lines on the pavements. How they came to be there, I still do not know. The only reason I can think of is that sailors threw them in the sea when they were broken. They must have been discarded years ago and so they were of great interest to me.

We were lucky children as a park backed onto the end of our garden and although a great deal of poverty existed in the East End, children were never short of parks. There was Greenwich Park with Plum Pudding Hill and Island Gardens where the large domed entrance to the foot tunnel was situated. There was also Blackheath and Kidmore, but they were too far away to go to alone.

We lived in Stebondale Street, which led to Island Gardens. The park was home to a round iron lift built in Victorian times. A ride down the lift and a walk through the tunnel and then up another lift and you would arrive in Greenwich. Sometimes, I would play a game with myself imagining that the tunnel suddenly cracked and the river came rushing in and I would run quickly through the tunnel in order not to drown. White glazed tiles covered the tunnel's curved walls, which were always wet with condensation; I used to think this was the river seeping through. We would shout while running through the tunnel so we could hear the hollow sound and the echo of our voices. I can still hear the noise of the gates as they closed. It was all so exciting and the use of the tunnel was free for everyone, and still is today.

Greenwich is of course famous all over the world—Greenwich Meridian, Greenwich Mean Time and the fact that Queen Elizabeth I resided there. I remember Greenwich Park and the worn brass handles that gave a measure of some sort, but I can't remember what it represented. I only know we always tried to stretch our arms to cover the space. I bet the brass handles are still there. Not far from Greenwich is Blackheath, which was a very special place on account of the big fair that took place once a year.

In those days you could win really big prizes. We would leave home when it was dark and the fair would be lit up like fairyland. Mum and Dad would give us sixpence to spend, which was a lot of money. This was a special treat and we were able to afford lots of rides and played on the glass cabinets with little electric cranes inside them. We would try to manoeuvre the cranes to pick up one of the gleaming prizes that lay amongst the jellybeans. It was all a matter of skill, but we were never lucky.

Mum and Dad would join us on the rides. They had married in their teens and were still very young and enjoyed the fair as much as we did. It was good to see them happy, as I knew it was hard sometimes for Dad to provide for us all. Women stayed home and looked after the house and family in those days, so there was only one breadwinner and there were times when life could be hard. Fairs such as those I knew as a child do not seem to be around any more and those today do not offer the big prizes that were there years ago. A plastic toy of little worth will not make a child's eyes light up as ours did. It is very sad that children today have no knowledge of the wonderful fairs of bygone days which gave such pleasure to many children who lived dull and drab lives.

Many children lived with fathers who came home drunk, spending more on drink than they gave their wives to live on. They would cause havoc and violence in the home and produce baby after baby which they could not afford to keep. Older children were often forced to live out their childhoods as drudges, cleaning and helping the poor mothers look after the little ones, sometimes having to miss school if their mother became sick. For many children a lively imagination was the only way they could add colour to their lives. I believe that it is due to the use of the imagination that the East End of London produced so many well-known writers and theatrical personalities.

Our house was a rented, double-fronted shop. The living area was behind the shop and the bedrooms were upstairs. There was no bathroom; you washed in the kitchen and bathed in a galvanized bathtub on a Friday night. There was an outside toilet and yard and at the bottom of the yard was a fence. When older, many went to the local public baths where you paid and would be given a towel. You were allowed a certain amount of time and if you overstayed, the attendant would knock on the door and shout "Get out!" and you would rush and dry quickly. The bottom of our garden looked onto a park—and what a park it was! There was a recreation ground for football, a big open-air swimming pool, a playground with swings, slides, roundabouts and a sandpit. In another area were tennis courts and a big grass area where girls would dress up and play May Queen on May Day and have picnics after school. In the summer holidays we would play out all day long. We never thought about being in danger as children do today, and so we kept our childish innocence a little longer. Of course, we were told not to speak to strangers; this was drummed into us regularly.

On cold winter nights, friends would play 'I Spy', looking in the shop windows near us. We lived in the middle of a row of six shops. At the corner, near the entrance to the park was Mrs Kirk's shop. This was our shop for sweets and groceries, although she never sold the unsalted butter Mum liked and I used to go to a shop further along our street to get that. Every season had its games. Whipping top, hopscotch, marbles, roller skates, cigarette card swapping, hula-hoop, yo-yos and too many more to mention. I cannot remember any child ever saying they were bored.

There was a pub on the corner of the other side of the park entrance and I used to love to lie in my bed and listen to people singing on a Saturday night on their way home after the pub had closed. They would sing the songs Mum and Dad sang with us on a Sunday evening. Some would be drunk, but they all sounded happy. My parents never went to the pub, but would have a drink at home with friends or family when it was a special occasion. They used to think it was shocking to see children outside the pub while their Mums and Dads were inside drinking. This was a part of East End life, and one that many children grew up with and accepted. So long as they had a packet of crisps and lemonade while they waited, they didn't seem to care.

With my bedroom facing the street, I felt comforted by the light of the buses as they passed our house. Their headlights would move across the room as the bus went by. Because I was afraid of the dark I would imagine all sorts of horrible creatures lurking in my bedroom. The bus passing would comfort me and make me feel less afraid. I would lie awake and when the last bus had gone all would be still and quiet. My brothers would have been asleep for ages and I would hear Mum and Dad come upstairs. They always kissed each other goodnight, which I could hear, after which I knew I was all alone. Some nights a mist would cover the area and the boats would sound their foghorns, which made the atmosphere even more eerie. I would lie awake and sometimes morning would arrive and I had not slept, or so it seemed at the time. I never told Mum about this, but it was a very bad time for me.

Some nights the toffee apple man would come round the streets, always walking in the middle of the road with his barrow. We would hear him call, "Two a penny toffee apples", just after we children were tucked up in bed. Mum would get cross when we would call out, "Can we have a toffee apple please Mum?" "No! You can't. It's not good for your teeth," was her usual reply, although she did surprise us a few times and brought one up to us.

His call was so loud we couldn't miss him, but why did he have to come so late we wondered? At times during the holidays a man would come round the streets with a horse and cart. It was only a little horse and on top of the cart he had a roundabout which was also small. It could fit eight children squashed together on the little seats. We had to climb up a little wooden ladder to sit on the seats while he turned the roundabout with his hand and we would go. The ride did not last very long but we all loved it. An empty jam jar was the price for a ride and we would rush to get as many jars as we could from relatives and neighbours before he moved further down the street. I often wondered why he wanted the empty jars but I never asked and so I never found out.

The Isle of Dogs was made up of many nationalities and religions. People helped each other and if the man of the house was sick and could not work, or when the mother was ill and the children needed care, everyone mucked in and no family was left in trouble. If a man was very drunk and violent there would be men from other families who would go and 'sort him out'. It was a close-knit community and looking back I feel privileged to have been a part of that life and have had the opportunity to experience the spirit that existed in the East End at that time. It made me grow up understanding what poverty and social inequality does to people and how unfair life can be for some.

Around Easter time, Irish Catholics would make a display of Jesus and Mary with candles and flowers in the windows of an upstairs room. The displays would be draped with lace and the windows looked like beautiful framed pictures. The Priest walked around the streets and blessed the houses, swinging a container of sweet-smelling incense. Some of the children would follow the priest from street to street, stopping to look at the wonderful window displays, which were lit up like fairy grottos. Well, as I imagined a fairy grotto would look. It was all very exciting.

When Good Friday came around a couple of the older girls would take a big thick barge rope, extend it from one side of the road to the other and use it as a skipping rope. The grown-up married women would take it in turns to hold the rope, as it was very heavy. Everyone would be expected to jump in as the rope was turning. This would go on along all the streets, not just ours, and it was a sight to behold with all the mothers and aunts jumping in and having their turn.

I was about eight when we came to live in Stebondale Street on the Island. Recently, I read in one of the Island Trust magazines that Stebondale was one of the island's worst hit streets during the war. Every day brought a new scene for us.

Beautiful draught horses hauled heavy barrels of beer from Whitbread's Brewery. You could not help but stare in wonder at these beautiful animals, which were always so well groomed and handsome. Tall horses with enormous hooves and drays reaching high up into the air, so high we had to crane our necks to see the drivers. The drays were always driven by big, strapping men who wore leather aprons and sat proudly holding the reins, guiding their charges.

The horses had great leather halters round their necks and their manes were plaited and knotted with coloured ribbon. The leather straps around their necks were covered with ornamental brass emblems. These horse brasses are now bought by people to display in their homes. The originals are very collectible and it must be something to hold an authentic brass, knowing that at one time a beautiful draught horse wore it proudly, and its owner polished it with love.

Our street was paved with cobblestones when we first came to live there, and I loved to listen to the sound of horses' hooves on them and see such large animals trotting so gracefully while carrying such heavy loads. Sometimes they would leave droppings on the road and it was commonplace to see someone rushing with a bucket and shovel to collect them. This was not to make the road clean but for the manure to use on their allotment. Sadly these horses are no longer seen on the streets of the East End, and are mostly just seen on special occasions like the Great British Beer Festival at Earls Court. These wonderful scenes that were free for me to enjoy as a child now live only in my memory. How I would love my children and grandchildren to share these pictures. I hope that through my writing I will be able to conjure up the scenes of my childhood for them.

Sometimes buskers, hoping to earn a bob or two, would walk

in the road dressed up and playing an instrument to entertain us. I remember my Mum's reaction when two men dressed as women came along one day. "They are Aunt Sallies," she said, "Don't look at them. Come indoors!" I never knew why she said this and still don't know to this day. I asked my Aunt Con about it one day and she said my Grandma used to say the same thing to her, but she never knew what she meant by it either.

I used to love to entertain the local children. They would sit on the pavement and I would dress up, dance and sing for them. I loved the films and grew up with Fred Astaire, Ginger Rogers and all the wonderful Ziegfeld showgirls who could be seen at the cinema in those days. You would see the main picture, then a B-Movie and during the interval an enormous Wurlitzer electric organ would rise up slowly from below the stage. The organ was white and glowed with multi-coloured lights and the organist wore a white suit. With a microphone beside him he would announce the songs he would play. The organist would end with his signature tune and wave. As the organ slowly descended back down below the stage you could hear the music slowly fading. Outings to the cinema with Mum and Dad in those days were magical.

During this entertainment the audience would have the opportunity to buy ice cream and sweets from girls with their goods hung on a tray by a strap round their neck. They wore white overalls with little caps and always looked clean and smart. Getting into the cinema wasn't always easy; sometimes people would have to queue for a long time, especially if it was a good film and a Saturday night. The evening could end with disappointment if a sign suddenly appeared in front of the queue informing the public that all the sixpenny-and-one-shilling seats were now sold out. The cinema attendant would call out, "Sorry, no more seats, but there are some left in the one and sixpence." Some people would move over to the shorter queue and would stand in front of the sign that read 'one shilling and sixpence', but often for our family of six the difference was too much and we would all go home feeling disappointed.

After watching a show I would be full of thoughts of how much I would love to be an entertainer like the organist or a film star and dream of all the wonderful things I could do. At ten years of age everything seemed possible and that is the way I used to think. The world was my oyster, I told myself; all I had to do was to grow up. But I was not grown-up yet and the next best thing I could do was pretend to be and entertain my friends. So I'd sing, "When the Poppies Bloom Again" at the top of my voice, wearing my red tap shoes with some old lace curtains draped around me. I would sing and dance imagining I was Ginger Rogers or Judy Garland and the children would sit on the cold stone pavement just to watch me.

Star-struck is what I was, but I was not alone, as a lot of little girls felt the same way. This was a time when film stars dressed beautifully and wouldn't be seen unless they were made-up and wearing the very latest fashions. Photos would show them smiling, looking glamorous, with beautiful furs draped around them and jewellery worn to excess. This was the way it was, fashion from head-to-toe: hats, matching gloves, handbags, shoes, and never a hair out of place.

This was also the time of the Eugene Permanent Wave machine, fabulous furs, powder puffs, compacts, elegant cigarette holders and silk stockings. Nylon had not been invented yet and it was pure silk stockings for those who could afford them or lisle stockings for those who had to make them last. People tried to present themselves with a good image and I loved to see my good-looking, tall mother dressed-up smart, and looking like a film star. Of course, how you dressed made an impression in those days, and it is a sad reflection to know that the poor were already being stigmatized by what they wore.

Mum was very conscious of cleanliness and I can recall the day when she called me to the window, then, with an air of secrecy, opened the curtain and told me to watch. "See that man selling the candy floss. Well you watch him. See how he has just licked his fingers and is now touching the floss which he is selling to that child. Can you understand why I do not want you to buy that stuff from him?" That picture was worth more than a thousand words to me. Mum was clever; I knew that. I dare not think what she would have said if she had found out about the locust we ate off the ground.

I passed the exam to get into a grammar school. To get to my school in Millwall it was necessary to take a bus over a bridge. This was an enormous swing bridge which opened to let the ships pass through. Many times our bus would have to wait while a big ship passed. Sometimes there was more than one ship, and this would make us very late for school. It was not a serious problem as teachers were used to this happening. All we had to say when we arrived late at school was, "Sorry Miss, we had a Bridger." If we saw that there was going to be a very long delay we would get off the bus and walk along the docks, cross a bridge further down which had not yet been opened and finish our journey to school on foot.

I was really happy at Millwall Central School because at last I was free from the name-calling I had suffered at my other school. "Chinese eyes, Chinese eyes" is what the children would call after me. The bullying spoiled those early years, but somehow I still managed to do well at school, considering how unhappy I was. My parents were very proud of me and they saw I was a good student and always did my best. My marks and position in exams was always very good and once I came top of my class. I was very happy and proud of my new school and I looked forward to being free to study without having to cope with the unkindness I had been subjected to.

My summer uniform was a Panama straw hat with a blue-and-white gingham dress, a navy blue blazer, white ankle socks and black shoes. In the winter, I wore a navy blue velour hat, matching gabardine coat, a striped blue and white tie, navy blue gym slip and a white blouse. Around my waist I wore a girdle that matched my tie. Black woollen stockings and black shoes completed the school's regulation uniform, and I felt proud and privileged to wear it. The school emblem was an enamel badge with the design of a windmill.

I can remember being very worried the night before I started my new school. Mum and Dad had fulfilled all the requirements laid down by it. I had a brown leather satchel and my name was written inside it in ink with all the necessary equipment inside. However, there was one thing missing: a fountain pen. I had wanted so much to have a Conway Stewart Dinkie small fountain pen. I am sure had I asked Mum and Dad they would have got one for me, but instead I was given a big fountain pen the night before I started school. I was so worried I would not have a pen at all that it was a relief when I was given one. In those days, children were aware of the financial strain it was for parents to buy their school uniform, so they did not ask for a special sort of pen. We could not be disappointed about anything for long, as we were taught to appreciate and be thankful for what we were given. I counted my blessings and the little pen I had wanted so much was soon forgotten.

French lessons were a breeze and I learned very quickly; I had a flare for the language, so I was told. I remember after the first few days at school one girl asked me if I could roll my Rs. I thought she said roll my eyes. It was quite funny when I said "Yes", and proceeded to roll my eyes. This made us laugh and I have never forgotten it. I enjoyed indoor sports and was made vice-captain of the team.

At my previous school I had been chosen to swim in the London Schools Swimming Gala. I swam breaststroke and won a bronze medal. I was a good swimmer, having already had three life saving certificates by the age of ten.

My aunt came to watch me with Mum and Dad. She and my uncle were so pleased with me that a few days later they took me across the water to Peckham Market and told me to choose whichever doll I liked. I chose one that was not very expensive and they told me to choose another. "It doesn't matter how much it costs," I was told. We had been brought up not to be greedy, so I stuck to the one I had chosen, even though there were dolls that were much more beautiful. I was about ten at that time. I called my doll 'Rosebud' and my uncle made me a rocking cradle for it. I used to have the cradle at the bottom of my bed with a piece of string tied to it and the head of my bed. I would pull the string gently as I was going to sleep and rock the cradle.

I loved babies and my life would have been ruined if I had found that, like some women, I was unable to have children. (Happily, I married and had two sons and a daughter, but that's another story).

After a while, Mum decided that I was too old to carry a doll around and looked silly because I was now growing fast and was very tall for my age. Without my knowledge, she gave Rosebud to a cousin I didn't like. One day I saw Rosebud lying in my gran's Airey with her head off. I think Mum would be upset if she had known how much this hurt me.

Going away for summer holidays was not a typical part of East End life in those days. We were lucky children though because we were taken on day trips of a Sunday. Quite a lot of the community went on holiday once a year to go hop-picking in Kent. That way they earned money and also got away to the country. Big lorries collected families and off they went, returning a week later with big green apples to give to their friends. I had never seen such big apples in the shops.

Trips to Southend-on-Sea were a real treat for us. We went there on a big steam train. The smell of the train's smoke lingers in my memory and makes me relive those times as if they were happening now. Mum would be dressed-up smart with high heels that by the end of the day were crippling her feet so that she could hardly walk. This was something Mum always did because new shoes were part of the fashionable image she was obliged to portray. She was not alone in this as so many women did the same and because of this have suffered with bunions and bad feet for the rest of their lives.

When the tide was out, there was mud instead of sand and this was really something to see. A mile of mud to walk through to reach the sea, but we children never minded. You could smell the strong salty air and there were cockles and winkles, soft ice cream and the fun fair on the famous Southend Pier, and after that the ride home on the train. What more could a child ask for? Who cared about the mud?

I have memories of days out going by bus and riding into the country with Mum and Dad. I must not forget to mention the Sunday trips to Hyde Park where Mum and Dad could listen to the soapbox orators. That was the time when Oswald Mosley and his Blackshirts were spreading the word of Fascism around the East End. In 1936 there was the Battle of Cable Street: a clash between the Metropolitan Police overseeing a march by the British Union of Fascists and anti-fascists made up of local Jewish, socialist, anarchists and Irish groups. Most working class people were politically minded in those days and rightly so, for they had little to lose, but much to gain if the right party came to power.

Another of our famous London parks was Regent's Park, which housed London Zoo. On other Sundays we would go to Hampstead Heath. Some Sundays we would all be dressed in our best clothes to visit our paternal grandparents. They had an antiques shop at one time and I used to be fascinated by some of the ornaments and furniture in their home.

I loved those visits because all the brothers, sisters and their families would be there. It was good to see Mum and Dad laughing, joking and also having heated political discussions. We children would play with our cousins and I would feel very happy. It would be late at night when we finally left and we would fall asleep on the bus going home.

We had many Sunday trips and I think we were very fortunate children because all those outings cost money. We had our first real holiday in August 1939. This was to be for two weeks with Mum, Aunt Con and Grandma. Dad was to visit at weekends. We went to Basildon, but war was imminent and Dad thought we should all return before the two weeks were up. So that was the end of our holiday.

We were fortunate to have our extended family living nearby. This allowed us to grow up feeling secure and protected. Aunt Con, Mum's youngest sister, lived a few houses along the road. She was only ten years older than me, so she was more like a sister. She married at nineteen and seemed to be well off as she was always buying expensive food, such as mushrooms and cream cakes. Mum did not buy cakes, but made them herself. They were lovely but the cream cakes Aunt Con bought were so much better.

I was born on my Grandma's fiftieth birthday and I was her first grandchild. Maybe that is why I always felt such a strong bond with her. Grandma would never put on the gaslight till it got very dark. She was left a widow with seven children when she was forty-two and had learned to live on a very tight budget. We would sit in the glow of the firelight. I would talk and she would listen. There was a black stove with a kettle always on top of it, steaming away, ready for a cup of tea for whoever called. I loved my Grandma and I really enjoyed being with her. I would sit and watch her comb her long grey hair, and when she had finished she would take the hair that was in the comb, hold it in her fingers and twist it into string. With this she would tie the end of her plait to stop it from unwinding. Then she would wind the plait round and round the back of her head and with large hairpins she would fasten it into place. While she did this, the curling tongs would be heating on the gas ring. Holding them near to her face she would test their heat and when she felt they were the right temperature she curled her short fringe. This daily ritual would be in readiness for her youngest son, my Uncle Bill, coming home from work. Most men of his age were married in those days but he was the breadwinner and needed to help Gran.

Hair done, it was time for her daily change of overalls. This was always prettily printed cotton, which crossed over and folded across her big tummy and was tied at the back. Poor Gran had bad feet and wore black plimsolls. After all these preparations had been completed, Gran was ready to sit in her chair, resting and reading the evening paper, The Star.

This was her time, and she deserved every minute of it.

At one end of the room was an old organ and sometimes my Aunt Con would play it and sing. She was really good and she and my Mum had fine singing voices. Granddad, who died before I was born, was supposed to have been a great pianist who played and sang all over London. He was a ladies' man so I have been told, and would be out all the time, working by day on the wharves and out all night, leaving my poor Grandma at home with the children. He was a bully and a drunk like a lot of men were in those days. Mum used to say that she wished he was still alive so she could give him a piece of her mind.

Grandma had a very hard life with him by all accounts and I used to feel very sorry for her when I looked at her stooped figure and the plimsolls on her poor feet. She had no real enjoyment out of life, especially as one of her beloved twin daughters had died at twenty-one. How could she live through such trauma and be so nice? This set an example for me, which I have always tried to follow. I often wonder if Gran knows what an important part she played in my life. I would like to think she does.

Every Saturday I would do her weekend shopping and she would give me a penny for doing so. Running errands was the way we children were able to save up and buy birthday and Christmas presents for her, Mum and Dad.

One day I tore my new best Sunday coat while climbing over a high fence at the Mudchute, another of the Isle of Dogs' large parks. I ran to Grandma and she sewed it for me so Mum would not know and I could avoid a telling off. Later, I realised Mum must have known because the sewing was not very good and you could see it a mile off, but Mum never said a word and I think Grandma must have warned her not to say anything. That was my Gran!

Grandmas had a very special place in those days and provided security when children felt parents had been unjust or did not love them. I always knew that my Grandma understood, whatever the problem was. She would tease me about my long legs and say, "You will catch your legs in your dress if you are not careful." Seeing as my dress was short this was quite a joke.

One day I saw a pair of brown brogue shoes in a shop window at Greenwich. I asked Mum if I could have them and she gave me the money to go "over the water" and buy them. I was so thrilled and showed them to Grandma, who said, "That is the first sensible pair of shoes I have ever seen on your feet." You can imagine how happy that made me. I think Mum used to put me into ankle strap black patent shoes. I do not think she considered a brogue shoe fashionable at that time. My Mum was a very smart and fashion-conscious young woman; she was good-looking, tall and slim. I was very proud whenever she came to my school as she always stood out from the other mothers.

I realise now that she was only young then. She was twenty-nine when I was ten. I never thought of her as young, which is sad really, but then she was my Mum and that was all that counted. Most children never seem to care or know how old their parents are.

Now my Gran was always old, though looking back I realise she was only fifty-eight when we first came to live near her. A hard life does show, that's for sure. She had lived on the Island for many years and was just a few houses away from us. Of course it was rented, as most houses were, and she had a living room in the Airey which was down a few steps and under the house. It never saw much daylight or sun. On nice days people who lived in Aireys would lean on the railings at the top of the steps and watch people go by. Neighbours on their way to Mrs Kirk's shop would stop and have a chat. My Uncle Bill would be there on a Saturday morning and would ask me to get him some razor blades or a packet of cigarettes and I would go to Mrs Kirk's and earn a penny for going.

Grandma had the downstairs room and two bedrooms on the first floor and in the rest of the house there lived another family. At the back was a scullery where the washing was done in a copper. This worked by lighting a fire under it to heat the water and so the washing was boiled. The scullery always smelt of *Sunlight* soap and boiled beetroot. It had a damp stone floor and this is where Gran did her washing for all her family as well as the washing she took in to earn a few extra bob. One outdoor toilet served both families, but everyone had a 'jerry' under the bed for use at night. Gran had a hard life and died at eighty-six, having lived for twenty years with her youngest daughter and family in Reading. Sadly, my mother was full of remorse after Gran died. She cried as she told me how she would hide when she was little to avoid helping Gran. When she got older she realized how unkind she had been and sadly the guilt never left her. I am sure there are many children who carry some form of guilt in their later years, but as they were children one can forgive them.

With *Tootal* ties and pocket-handkerchiefs to match, my Dad was also a smart dresser. My parents loved going to the West End to see the latest shows and I was so pleased for them when they got all dressed up. I would feel very happy when they were going out to enjoy themselves. I was left in charge of my brothers when they went out, but Aunt Con and Gran were nearby if they were needed and Aunt Con would call and check on us every so often. She told me that once when she looked in I was dancing on the table with a friend watching me. I don't think Mum would have liked to know that.

Before the war, Mum and Dad owned a hardware shop and Dad had a business as a master builder and decorator. He was a true artist and the work he did was beautiful. I would go to a house where he was working and watch him. His graining and marbling looked so real and he was always praised for his work. I was very proud of him. In those days, you could not buy ready-mixed coloured paint, so Dad had to mix his own.

Watching my father work was a real joy and I loved to be with him. There came a day when everything in the shop had to be sold off cheaply. There were 'Ack-Ack' guns on the Mudchute. Whenever the guns went off, the blast would knock some of the china off the shelves, ending up broken on the floor. It became necessary to sell everything and close the shop. This was sad, as it was a thriving business and the sale of the stock brought little of its true value. I remember we sold toilet rolls, which were a very new product and were special, as everyone had used newspapers until then.

About this time, everything started to change. The effects of war with Germany were starting to be felt and children from all the schools in the London area were evacuated to different parts of the country. We never went away as my parents did not see the need and they did not want to be without us, so kept us at home.

The war had not affected us seriously yet. We carried our gas masks with us all the time and the windows had brown paper strips stuck on them to stop the glass from flying about in case of a blast. Blackout curtains were compulsory and everyone's windows had to be well covered so that not a chink of light could be seen. Air raid wardens walked the streets, checking that not a glimmer was showing anywhere.

Rationing had started and families had sons coming home on leave in the uniform of the services they joined. Some looked very smart and older girls would be seen walking proudly beside them.

With the schools closed and children evacuated, there were not many children left to play with. Mum decided she would try to give us a few lessons. Some of the other children who had stayed behind like us were invited to join in. This was fine for my young brothers, but was not good for me. Mum did her best, but I was learning algebra, geometry and French, and poor Mum had no knowledge of these subjects. Gradually my desire and thirst for knowledge began to fade, and with them went my confidence.

My parents must have realised it was not good for children to live this way, so it was decided we had to be evacuated. Mum wrote to Mrs Freeborn, the headmistress of the Cubitt Town Infants School which my three brothers attended, asking if we could be evacuated to Buscot Park where the school had been moved to. There was no way that Mum and Dad would allow us to be split up and so she asked for all four children to be together. This meant I was with infants. I asked Mum in later years where my school had been evacuated to, but this was something she could not remember.

But now, through the internet I have found out where my school was evacuated to and it was Chippen Camden in Gloucestershire.

There were three or four teachers at Buscot Park. Mr Wood was one of them. I remember him very well, and I can see his face as clearly as though I had seen him yesterday. There was a big lake and it was part of Buscot Park, Lord Farringdon's Estate. I can recall quite vividly one of the days when we were all swimming in the lake. I swam under the murky water and deliberately grabbed Mr Wood's leg for a joke. I thought I would scare him and make him think it was some monster fish. A monster fish in an English lake? I ask you!

But don't forget, this was a child with a lively imagination.

Mr Wood was a nice teacher and took it in good fun. Looking back now, I think it was really quite a cheeky thing to do to a teacher and I was lucky not to be told off, but the teachers were very nice to us and we liked them very much.

During this time I missed my parents. It was a very sad and hard time for me. My brothers slept at the gatehouse with the other boys, a large building at the entrance to the estate. The girls had their rooms at the top of the big house, with two girls to a room. The big house was Lord Farringdon's stately home, standing in acres of land. There were beautiful laid-out gardens, a swimming pool and tennis courts. We were told there was also a small theatre with seating for seventy, but none of us ever saw inside of it, so I do not know if it really existed. The top floor where the girls slept had been the servants' quarters, but most of those servants had been conscripted and were busy doing war work or were in the armed forces. The stables had been converted into a dining room and the walls were painted with frescoes. We sat at long trestle tables all joined together to have our meals and I think there were about thirty-five children living there. Just outside the stables there was a huge tree, it must have been an oak. Thick branches extended from it. Some of the children would sit on the lowest branch and sing songs while we waited for the dining room to open. Even though I missed my parents I can recall some very happy times at Buscot. I used to sit on a branch of the oak tree and sing of a morning and watch for my brothers coming from the gatehouse with the other boys. I used to check them over to see they had washed and were tidy. Nearly every time one of them had a hole in his sock. Darning socks was a never-ending chore. One day, as I was picking primroses in the woods, a group of children came running, shouting out to me, "Come quickly, your brothers Harry and Donald are drowning." I was frantic with worry and ran to the lake as fast as I could. There they were, my dear brothers, out in the middle of the lake in a boat that was leaking. I loved them very much and the idea of them drowning was too much for me. I thought of my poor parents, of how they would feel if they were told their sons had drowned. In my imagination they were already dead. I was in a dreadful state by the time I reached the lake. Out of breath, I stood and shouted at them as best I could. They were both laughing at me, provoking me by standing up in the boat and making it rock. It seemed an age had passed before they managed to get the boat back to the edge of the lake. Looking back now, I realize that it was not as serious as I had thought, but I suppose it gave the other children a bit of excitement and something to talk about. I was a very conscientious sister and would sit up in bed until late at night darning my brothers' socks. Mr Wood came once to tell me that I must turn the lights out, but he let me keep them on a little longer when he saw what I was doing.

Mum and Dad were upset when they heard about me darning socks, especially because I had not told them my brothers needed new ones. Times were hard, and I did not want to worry them. I felt responsible for my brothers' welfare, as Mum and Dad were not around to look after them. My duty as a sister was to see they were all right, and I took this very seriously. My brother, Harry, was ten then. Donald was nearly nine and Derek was six. I was thirteen. We had another scare and this one could have easily ended in real tragedy. One day, one of the little girls climbed outside the window of her bedroom on the top floor and walked out onto the parapet. She would have been about four years of age. A teacher, Mrs Alchurch, tried to coax her back in. She also tried to keep the rest of us calm while she leaned out of the window and tried to talk the child into coming back inside.

She had warned us to be very quiet and not make a sound. Mrs Alchurch managed to get the girl to turn round and walk back along the parapet. The teacher then grabbed her and pulled her into the room. The parapet was very narrow and that child was lucky not to have fallen.

The girls in the bedroom next to ours used to put notes onto a *Dinkie* clip, which was used to curl hair, and tie them to a long piece of string and throw it out of the window along the parapet. We grabbed the clip as it landed near our window. We wrote a note, attached it to the clip and sent it back. It was all very secretive and exciting; even though there was nothing special happening to us that was worth writing about. Sometimes we would go into Farringdon to see a film, accompanied by a couple of teachers. It was so good to walk along the quiet country road all in line. Often I called at the post office to collect parcels from my parents. They contained Mum's fairy cakes, sweets and pocket money. They were too big to carry all the way into Farringdon, so I would hide them in a roadside bush and collect them on my way back. My teacher congratulated me on my initiative, which made me feel very proud.

Water lilies on the lake and a waterfall were a joy to see. Buscot was a wonderful place for a child to live. There was a big nursery where a gardener grew the seeds he nursed into plants. These would be planted around the grounds in cultivated beds. I remember asking if I could buy one of the beautiful pansies which were growing in the nursery; they were the biggest pansies I had ever seen. I wanted to surprise Mum by presenting it to her as a gift, but when I was told it would cost two shillings and sixpence, I had to forget about it. Half a crown was too much money. Mr Buck was Lord Farringdon's secretary. We saw him strolling around the grounds. He seemed like a nice man and always said hello to us.

On special days we had bread and jam for tea. This was a real treat. I made the little blob of jam on my tea plate last and last. At jam tea we were allowed to have as much bread and margarine as we could eat. I made the most of it, leaving the table with the feeling of having had plenty of food, which was unusual during rationing. When I felt very hungry my Mum's fairy cakes were very welcome. I divided them equally to share with my brothers, but once I ate some before they knew the parcel had arrived. I never told them about this. I was too ashamed. What a horrible sister I was to do that. To think I stole from my little brothers. Guilt enveloped me and I knew I would never do such a thing again. I realise now that hunger could have been the only reason for my behaviour. When the next parcel came I gave my share to my brothers, then I felt better.

When Mum and Dad came to visit Buscot on a Sunday, they would take us out and we would have a lovely time. It was as it used to be. We were all together again as a family. My brothers and I needed that comfort. Lots of the parents arrived by coach. They would go to the local pub while the children waited outside for them. My parents came by themselves on a bus. Sometimes my uncle and aunt would be with them. I loved those times and remember the Anchor Inn where my parents took us for tea. It was owned by two brothers, their names were Eric and Douglas Cutts. It was a lovely country inn. Everything about it was special for me. Their homemade blackberry jam consisted mostly of whole berries. I have tried to make jam like it over the years but have never been successful. I ask myself now whether it really was that good, or was that just the way a hungry child remembers it? I can still taste and see that jam as I write and I am convinced it was special. We would go to Buscot village and Lechlade to buy sweets and post our letters. Looking back, I think we were allowed to go on our own after tea and before going to bed. I recall the evenings were always fine when we went out. It must have been summer time when we were evacuated. Once there was a dreadful commotion and the story went around that someone had put chewing gum in the service lift. The story went like this: A princess was dining with Lord Farringdon at the time. The butler had lifted a tray from the service lift which had glasses on it. Chewing gum was found stuck to the bottom of the tray. As the butler lifted the tray the gum made him need to pull hard, causing all the glasses to fall to the ground. Many were broken. The story could have been made up to stop children putting chewing gum in places where it shouldn't be. I never found out, but I did wonder. At the time I was very concerned, thinking one of my brothers could have done it. My imagination, as usual, ran riot and I was very worried. I thought about poor Mum and Dad having to pay for the broken glasses. I knew they would be very expensive because they belonged to a lord. Oh dear!

At bedtime, we would go quietly up the stairs all together, with a teacher in charge. As we went up those stairs we saw rooms leading off the landing. They looked so beautiful and luxurious, I imagined the many guests who must have visited Buscot and been entertained in them. For a child from the East End, it was quite something to see the beautiful peacocks and peahens strutting around the estate. I loved the look of them but hated the screeching sound they made. They were like a fantasy from one of my books. The book I loved most of all had black-and-white drawings in the style I know now to be William Morris. All my books were lost when our house was bombed. That was very sad for me. I have searched hoping to find one of these books. Sadly, I had no such luck. I can still feel the book's lovely thin paper. The pages felt like silk.

One day, my parents heard that all the children were going to be put into private homes in the nearby villages as a private girls school was going to be moved in. This upset my parents very much as they were socialists and considered this to be a slight on children from the working class area of the Isle of Dogs. I have recently learned a private girls school from Kent was moved in and there are photos of girls on bikes and playing tennis. None of these opportunities were available to us kids from the East End — which says a lot.

The possibility that the four of us would be separated would not suit my parents and so they took us back home to London.

We had not been home for long when the Blitz began in September 1940. It was a nightmare. There was the smell of burning everywhere. Water was pouring out from the mains, flooding the roads. Chemical factories were exploding. People walked about in a daze not knowing what to do. We listened to the constant drone of the German bombers as they blackened the skies, flying low, relentlessly dropping their heavy bombs over London. Their target was the docks. With the docks all ablaze and the sky glowing bright red it was easy for the planes to return the next night and follow the curve of the river. Inside the curve was the Isle of Dogs, all lit up, an easy target for the bombers. It was an awful feeling, knowing there were men up in the sky, intent on killing us. I imagined the faces of the pilots, their goggles, the leather uniforms they wore, and I was frightened. We all felt so tired during the day, having been woken up so many times in the night. We knew that whenever the sirens sounded, we had to get to the shelter quickly. To leave your lovely warm bed and go downstairs out into the cold night air and into the Anderson air raid shelter was no joke.

Dad had dug our shelter down into the ground. These shelters were sometimes referred to as 'dug outs'. It was at the bottom of the garden, covered with earth to camouflage it. Sometimes we were down there all night before the all-clear sounded. There were nights when we were forced to make the trip to the shelter three times. Just as we had settled down to sleep in the shelter, the all-clear would sound. We would trail back upstairs to bed. Then, just as we were getting off to sleep, warm and cosy, the siren would sound again. Down we would all go, back to the shelter in the garden.

I remember my mother asking once when we were down in the shelter, "Where is Donald?" Donald, who was always a heavy sleeper, had not followed us. That was very worrying and Dad had to go back and fetch him. A bomb could have dropped and they both could have been killed. We were among the lucky ones. Dad had painted the inside of our shelter with whitewash. Being a decorator he always made everything nice for us in the house and now the shelter was our house too. He did his best to make us comfortable. The whitewash made the place much brighter. When the candles were lit, it was nice and bright. I know a lot of shelters were very dark inside and were quite frightening to be in. It is surprising that we could even speak of being cozy and comfortable. Being together was the most important thing in the world at that time and the shelter offered a sense of security. That was until a bomb dropped so near us that we felt as though we had all been thrown up into the air, spun around and then put down again, shelter and all.

There was a night when we could hear heavy footsteps walking over the top of us. Dad was not with us. Mum and I were awake and frightened in case it was a German who had managed to get out after his plane had been knocked down. We sat there terrified until the footsteps died away. The next day we saw big footprints in the earth on top of the shelter. Someone said it could have been a scrounger. These were people who went searching in houses that had been bombed, taking the belongings that were left there.

At that time Dad was doing war work over the water. This meant he was across the river, on the other side of the Thames. When the sirens sounded, the tunnel was closed and Dad and many others were unable to get home. Mum used to be worried and because I was the eldest she shared her worries with me. We made sure my brothers were never troubled by our fears. They were little and had to be protected as much as possible. She would read to us from a novel *Sorrell and Son* by Warwick Deeping. It was a sad story, but a lovely one. I looked forward to Mum reading a piece each night but my brothers soon fell asleep. I was the only one listening to Mum after a little while. She also used to knit socks for my brothers in the candlelight and some nights we would all play guessing games until we were tired and fell asleep, exhausted.

My parents didn't wait too long to move out of the East End once they realised how determined the Germans were to destroy London, the Docks being their main target. We had all been under the illusion that the German planes would never be able to get through the barrage balloons that flew high in the sky over the city. Now we realised how wrong we had been. On one particular night, we went to see my father's parents to ask them to move away with us. They said they couldn't leave the rest of the family. That night on our way home the siren sounded earlier than usual. The streets were suddenly deserted. An air raid warden directed us into a public shelter under an electricity showroom in Poplar. It was already full with beds on the floor and people standing. We had no room to move. We were squashed together all night, standing in the same place. Suddenly there was an enormous crash. We could hear the sound of plaster falling. People started to rush to the exit but were turned back and told to keep calm. We waited for another loud bang, but it never came. All we could hear was a rumbling sound, which seemed to be all around us.

Early in the morning, after the all-clear had sounded, we walked to the bus stop to catch our bus home to the Island. We waited and waited. Mum began to get very cross because we were waiting such a long time and no bus had arrived. It was decided that we had better start walking. We were all tired and worn out from standing up for eight hours without sleep. As we walked through the familiar areas we realized the extent of the devastation that had taken place while we were down in the shelter. Houses were still burning; people were standing in groups, crying. Whole streets were gone. It was unbelievable. No one could imagine a bomb flattening a whole street of houses. This night was the start of the use of land mines. We walked through the devastation, passing the shells of houses that had stood tall the night before, wondering what we would find when we reached Stebondale Street. Would Gran and Uncle Bill be there? Would Aunt Con, Uncle Chris and their baby Terry be alright?

We wanted to get home and find the answers, but our legs were tired and it took ages to reach home that day. We were lucky. Our house had been bombed, but was not completely demolished and all our family were alive, but it was still a nightmare. The smell of burning was everywhere. Water was pouring out from the mains, flooding the roads. Chemical factories were still exploding. People were walking about in a daze, not knowing what to do. We saw people with blackened faces, crying because they had lost everything. The London Fire Service was working so hard, but they were worn out, having worked all night fighting blazes in the docks. These pictures remain so vividly in my memory.

Our cat, Ginger, had managed to survive the night. He came up to us, purring and wrapping himself around our feet. I picked him up and cried, burying my head in his fur. I cried for Ginger, for myself and for everyone. The worry of the bombers returning suddenly during the daytime was very frightening. This was always in my mind when people were standing around chatting. Didn't they realize that the planes could come again? Why were they outside in the street where they could be hit by planes swooping down to machine-gun them? What were they thinking of? I thought then that adults should show more sense. That night we slept in my Aunt Con's shelter. It was dark and claustrophobic. I stood outside with the grownups, watching the planes flying low in great numbers. You could see them so clearly as the whole sky and docks were lit up. It was like Guy Fawkes Night, with the noise of the bombs dropping and chemical factories exploding.

A few days later Dad made the decision that we had to leave in order to be safe. My mother's two sisters, May and Con, with their children and my maternal Grandmother came with us and the husbands left Dad to take care of us all, saying they would join us in a few days' time. My father's parents having refused to come with us and stayed, as many Londoners did, living through the whole of the bombing of London. They lived through the V-1 and V-2 flying bombs, sleeping every night in the nearest underground tube station till the war in Europe ended. Such bravery is written about in many books. It was a time of great fortitude and courage. A time when no one could think of tomorrow. We left with nothing. We were refugees from London. It was planned that we would all live at Buscot and we caught a train, intending to go there. It was late at night when the train stopped at Reading. We were all so tired and worn out that it was decided we should stay the night there.

My Aunt May and my parents had friends who lived there. They made up beds on the floor, gave us food and made us very welcome. I will never forget that night.

It was like another world and yet we were only forty miles from London. It was quiet and peaceful, almost unbelievable. There was not a sign of a war going on. No sirens sounded and we were able to sleep right through the night until the morning. It was on that night that I made myself a promise. I would in future always appreciate my bed and my sleep. Many years have passed and I still appreciate my sleep and a comfortable bed, for I can never forget the tiredness we suffered and the torture of not being allowed to have a full night's rest.

The next day the grownups decided that we would not go on to Buscot after all, but look for a house so that all the family could live together until each had found suitable accommodation. They found a large house. Mum had to take the top floor, as we were all older children. Every drop of water had to be brought up from three floors down. There were times when we had only coal dust to make a fire in the room. All our family had to sleep in one room and eat, cook and wash in the other. The toilet was downstairs in the garden. Dad was away working at Rochester and came home at weekends when he could.

Life was never the same again for me. My schooling had been so disrupted that when I was sent to E.P. Collier Grammar School in Reading I could not concentrate or remember anything. I did not know which was North, South, East or West. I did not know which was my right or my left, and the most ordinary simple things I had learned when in primary school had gone. All I could do was simple maths and this I did well. Children were unkind, as children will be, and again I suffered name-calling. This time it was "Evacuee". I was nearly fourteen when I started at the Reading school. I was put into a class lower than where I was at my school in Millwall. "Oh! You are an evacuee?" This was said as if I had something wrong with me. Children would call after me too. It all became too much and I begged my mother to let me leave school. I think she must have realised that I was no longer the keen, industrious student I had been and finally she went to the school and asked if they would release me. I was supposed to stay until I was sixteen, but by then I was fifteen and they allowed me to go.

Even though I was not happy at school I was certainly not ready to go out into the wide world to work. I had been playing cowboys and Indians with my brothers and still felt like a child. I know I felt very uncomfortable in my shoes that had Cuban heels, flesh-coloured stockings instead of black wool tights and curled hair. No more white ankle socks; no more school uniform. I had to grow up suddenly. Children adapt easily so they say, and I was one who did.

Soon I was into fashion, make-up, and curling my long thick chestnut hair into the latest styles, a skill that I developed a flair for. I was now grown up, and I had no idea it had happened. I had always thought I would feel different, with the world suddenly opening up, giving me the chance to do all the things I wanted to do and be all the things I wanted to be. But it was not like that at all. So the years passed by and the war ended. Reading became the place where my parents settled for the rest of their lives. Mum lived there until 2001, when she passed away aged 95. Even at 90, she still looked good and liked to present herself well. Every morning she made-up and put on her earrings. She cooked every day for herself and was still fussy about hygiene. Dad died nine years before Mum, and she missed him an awful lot.

Many years ago we returned to Buscot Park. The gardens and lake looked unkempt. The stately home was no longer stately. Everything seemed to be so much smaller than I remembered it to be. It was all very disappointing. The wonder it once held had gone and I was sad.

However, memories stay and I can still visualise the wild

primroses growing in the woods. I can hear and see the peacocks, and the bluebells are still tall and blue. The lake is as it was and the gardens with the water lilies in the pond are still beautiful. The enormous oak tree we used to swing on while waiting to be called for breakfast is still there. So I will not be sad for what no longer exists but I will close my eyes and reawaken the many scenes that made me happy as a child.

Since my visit, I am happy to write that Buscot Park has been restored. The gardens are well kept and it belongs to the National Trust. It is open to the public and well worth visiting.

The Anchor Inn, at Eaton Hastings held happy memories which I mention in my story. It was a very popular public house and campsite until it was destroyed in 1980 by a tragic fire. The National Trust, which owns the land, decided to let the site go back to nature. Traces of the foundations are all that remain.

My Mum!

Lorraine Harrington

It is the year 2000 and I am seventy-three. My husband Cy had died on March 29th. He was eighty-seven and lived a varied and interesting life. He was my second husband, and my life was so much better for knowing him. We enjoyed each other and were interested in the same things. We had twenty-one happy years together.

Like many women in such a situation, the loss was too much

to bear, and I did not know what I would do without him. Also, like many in the same situation, I did everything quickly and without too much thought.

It was important that I kept myself busy and tried not to think too much, so I decided to go to New Zealand. It was my brother Don's birthday on May 15th, and I would see my other brother Del and all the family. Being with family was what I needed.

I had a good time and I felt better when I returned to Australia three weeks later. Now I was home and had time to think. This would bring forth feelings of desolation and despair and I continuously faced the question of what my life would be like without Cy.

I decided to sell my unit, as I would not be able to afford the mortgage now that Cy had gone. I was lucky as I sold it myself without having to pay agents' fees. I sold the furniture with the unit and stored a few items I wanted to keep which could be sent to England if I decided to stay there. The rest I gave to the Cancer Research fund. I decided I would go to Melbourne and Sydney, visit family and friends, and then go to England. Once in England, I would make up my mind if I stayed there. This time I had no ties, no home and only myself to consider. My children and grandchildren lived in England and so did my elderly mother. I also had friends I wanted to see.

Over the years, I had visited them all regularly, but never had enough time to enjoy more than a few weeks with them as I had a business to run.

I had plenty of time now as I was alone but being without Cy was not a good feeling. Mum had told me that they were putting central heating in her house in October and asked if I could come and stay with her while it was being done. This gave me a reason to get things sorted out quickly. So, I sold my house and furniture and put a few belongings in store.

It was October when I arrived in Reading. It was the town where my parents had lived for almost sixty years. The sun was shining, and I could smell the familiar smell of autumn. Memories flooded back and I thought of the time when I was fourteen.

We were evacuees when we went to live in Reading and had left behind our home in the East End of London. We lived on the Isle of Dogs, which was surrounded by the river Thames.

It was the time of the London Blitz. The sky was bright red, the docks were alight and burning, and the German bombers had a good view of the Thames, which they could follow and drop their bombs onto the docks and the surrounding streets and houses. People were dead and dying and all the time the sirens would sound announcing another air raid. The fear of not knowing what would happen was frightening.

I remember Mum reading to us when we were in the air raid shelter. The story was *Sorrel and Son* by Warwick Deeping and I enjoyed it so much. Mum also knitted socks for my brothers. I can see her now with the wool and four needles. Mum was not clever at making clothes and her cooking skills were very ordinary, but we loved what we were given to eat.

Dad was doing war work in Rochester, so he was not with us all the time, but it became too dangerous for us to stay and so Dad decided we had to leave.

Dad was in charge. My uncles had to stay but would come later. A train ride to Reading. Only forty miles from London is all it was and yet it felt like another world. We arrived at the station late at night and with us were my grandma, Aunt May and her son Billy, Aunt Con with her little boy Terry, Mum, Dad, my three brothers and me.

We went to stay with Aunt May's friends who were expecting us. There was no sound of bombs exploding, no sound of the hum of German planes overhead, and not the sound of a siren warning us to leave our warm beds and go down into the cold air raid shelter.

It was wonderful, and I will never forget the wonderful feeling of sleeping on a mattress on the floor, all cozy and warm. I knew that for the rest of my life I would always enjoy the pleasure of a nice warm comfortable bed and remember the kindness of the family who took us in and made us welcome.

Mum was eighteen-and-a-half when she married Dad, who was a year older.

They eloped and were married with two strangers brought in off the street as witnesses. When they left the registry office, Mum went home to tell her mother she was married, and Dad went home to tell his parents.

Both their families were related and were against them seeing each other. Mum and Dad were second cousins and very much in love. I understand they each stayed with their parents as single until they could find a place to rent. The family rallied round and helped, and I was born a year later. By the time Mum was twenty-seven, I had three brothers.

My Mum!

Mum was called Violet, and I was named after her. I was called "Little Vi" when little then "Young Vi" as I grew older. Mum and Dad endured a love-hate relationship which lasted sixty-four years with neither of them ever wanting someone else, although they were always saying they were going to divorce.

Sadly, Dad was a compulsive gambler, and this made life hard for all of us. Dad died five years before and Mum was now on her own and missing him dreadfully.

Mum was a woman of the old school, who considered, pride, loyalty, dignity, honesty, and good manners an essential part of life and thought people who were rude or disrespectful, and those who lied and cheated, were unacceptable.

She was the typical matriarch who ruled her children with a rod of iron. One look from Mum and we were stopped in our tracks from whatever we were doing. There was no need to question if we had done something that did not meet with her approval. That look said it all. Even so, we all knew we could always turn to Mum if we had any troubles and there were many times when we did.

She never said she loved us. Somehow, it was something she could not bring herself to say, but we all knew she did.

Well as I began, it is October, and I am back in the house I knew when I was fourteen. A lot has happened in the years since then. Sadly, my dad is no longer with us and I have just arrived from Australia to stay with Mum who is now ninety-three years of age.

It was good to be with Mum even though it was dark, cold,

and raining in England. Not a bit like the hot sunshine and blue skies I had left. Mum was so happy to see me, as I was to see her. I had last seen her two years before, but there was a change, and she was using a walking frame to get around the house and was now much thinner.

The days went by and one day Mum decided we should look at old photos. They were kept in a lovely old wooden box that at one time had been a music box.

Inside, there were photos and lots of lovely cards that Dad had given Mum on special occasions. They were beautiful cards, and the verses said a lot, but Dad was always able to write better words to express his love for Mum. We were both crying as we read the cards and I felt the need to cuddle Mum.

Holding her close was like cuddling an ironing board. She held herself so straight and stiff, but I was determined to make her loosen up.

"Cuddle me," I said, "For God's sake Mum, loosen up and cuddle me." She did and it was so good. From then on, she relaxed and found she could tell all her children she loved them, something she had not been able to do before.

It was quite a long time before she told me that she felt happy when she was able to do this. "I could never tell Dad I loved him," she said. "I wish I had now."

I thought that was very sad and I was quite shocked, but I later learned many women were like Mum. It was a symptom of the times they lived in and sadly so many women and men found it hard to say the words, "I love you". Now times have changed and today "Love Yaa" is used too freely and very often with little or no meaning. At least when Mum said she loved you, you knew she really meant it.

It was wonderful to hear her on the phone to New Zealand talking to her sons and saying, "Goodbye, I love you son". I saw her pleasure when she said this and it was good, but there was still a hard streak.

Once when I was down and cried because I missed Cy, she said, "Don't be so selfish. You wouldn't want him to have gone on with cancer and suffer more would you?"

"Of course not," I said.

"So, stop crying," was her answer. I could have done with a cuddle and some understanding, but that was my mum.

Mum came from a working-class background and had standards that had been instilled in her by her mother. My grandmother was left a widow at forty-one with seven children to bring up. I can see her now, holding out her hand with her exceptionally long fingers and touching the tip of her thumb with her forefinger and saying, "I have never owed anyone that much."

She was an independent woman who had a very hard life. Like Mum, you knew where you stood with Gran, and like Mum, you knew she loved you even though she never said so. You also knew you could rely on her to stand by you if you were right but expect no help if you lied or tried to cheat. So, I grew up with this background and took it all for granted, that everyone lived by these standards. Sadly, I have now found that this is not so.

A few weeks after I arrived, Mum was ill and so my brother who lived nearby and I took her to see a specialist. I was worried as I thought she could have cancer. I told her I would stay with her until the end if she had a serious illness. Fortunately, this was not the case, but she was unwell and one night I threw the single mattress from my bed upstairs over the landing, down the stairs and dragged it to the front room where Mum slept, and I slept on the floor next to her.

Mum woke up a few times and I gave her medication. I had a few tablets of low dose morphine that Cy had been taking for his cancer and I gave Mum one. She went back to sleep without pain, but a few hours later I had to call the doctor as she woke again in discomfort.

I told him about the morphine I had given to Mum, and he said that was OK. Mum would sometimes ask me for one of the little brown tablets and I would give her one when she was in pain. A week later she got better, and I went back upstairs to sleep and never had to give her any more tablets. It was lovely to be with Mum and I cherish the time we had together.

I had my computer in her front room where she now had her bed. At nighttime, when she was in bed, I would play music to her from my computer, and we would sing together as we did years ago when all the family joined in and sang on a Sunday night. We sang lots of the old songs she knew and loved, and we shared memories of Vera Lynn and the war years.

I bought a Max Bygrave's CD and played it, but she said it was not the same voice she had been used to and I think she was right. She would have been surprised if she knew that later I lived not far from him in Australia and my hairdresser's mother was his wife's sister.

Mum loved Scrabble and was very good at it, so we played

during the day. One day, I asked her doctor if he could give her something to stop her being agitated as she very often was. She would push her walker past me in a hurry to get to the toilet and get so agitated. I understood this, but she was always so upset and angry. He gave me a prescription and I gave Mum one of the tablets, but she was like a zombie. When we played scrabble, she was so slow and did not know what she was doing. "This is not the Mum I know," I told myself. I could not have my lively Mum who had such a good mind be this way, so I did not give her any more tablets. I would shop and buy nice food and make meals which she enjoyed. It was a wonderful time for me to have Mum to myself. She used to tell me that I was a good daughter, and she would look after me when she had gone. This was funny, as Mum and Dad were both atheists, but we all kissed goodnight, even from childhood and said, "God bless you". Crazy family!

My brothers from New Zealand wanted to visit her, but she told me she could not bear them to see her the way she was. Poor Mum was incontinent and had not left the house for six years. Although she was embarrassed by her daughter helping her when she had an accident, having her sons see her this way would be too much for her. I understood how she felt, but I don't know if my brothers did.

In December, Mum fell and broke three ribs. She was in pain and sat in her dressing gown all day. I looked after her with her home carer but after three weeks, I could see she was not going to get dressed and make herself up as she used to do. This was not good, and the doctor told me I had to try to get her to dress. I knew it was important, so I decided that the next day I would make a stand. I laid Mum's clothes out already for the carer to help her dress herself, but Mum was adamant.

She said there was no way she was going to be told what to do and be treated like a child; no one was going to dictate to her. She was not going to get dressed and that was that. She would dress when she felt like it and when she was ready.

I started to get angry, but she gave me that look that I knew so well from childhood and had not seen for years. It was the look that used to make me tremble, but not anymore. "Don't you look at me like that," I said. "I am not a child, but a grown woman and that look won't work with me anymore."

Then, suddenly, I saw a look in my mother's eyes I had never seen before. There was a look of fear as if she felt cowed. I felt dreadful and I realized I could not do this to my Mum.

The reversal of the mother-daughter role was not for me. So, I gave my mother back her dignity and allowed her to believe she was still the matriarchal figure she had always been.

"Ok Mum," I said. "Don't dress today, do it when you want to."

"So what?" I told myself, "If she doesn't want to dress, then she can stay as she is. It is her choice, and she is not harming anyone." So that was the end of trying to get Mum to do what I thought was best for her.

The next day, she said she did not feel well, and I thought, "Here she goes, acting up again like she used to when I was young." But as it happened, she really was ill and had to go into hospital. That was the start of my mother's decline. After ten days in hospital, she discharged herself. She was determined to go home. "If you won't take me home, I will pay someone to get me a taxi," she said. I knew Mum would do that and it was hard, but I managed to get her to stay until a doctor officially discharged her. The doctor asked her questions to check that she could cope, as was usual. Mum answered them all correctly and ended by asking the doctor, in a harsh tone, "Did you think I was mental?"

When we got home, she cried as she told me how she had been neglected. It was pitiful to see my Mum cry and the story she told me made me very sad. She said that she was treated so badly and that they had taken away every ounce of dignity she had left, and she wanted me to write a letter of complaint to the hospital. Her major concern was that by speaking out she could help others. "Some of the poor patients have no family who can speak up for them," she said. "I am lucky, I have you." Mum was a fighter! She would speak her mind regardless. She was a great one for justice. Not just for herself and her family, but for everyone. I knew she was telling the truth and I believed what she told me. So, I wrote a letter of complaint to the hospital.

She then said she would like the papers to know how old people were being treated and would I write to the local newspaper.

Being Mum's daughter, I had been brought up to fight for justice, so I wrote to the local paper. Mum had a bad accident when she was sixteen. She had beautiful, long, thick hair but after the accident she lost a lot of it. It grew back but was very thin and sparse. This was a cause of great sadness in Mum's life. It was once suggested to her that she wear wig, but in those days, wigs were so poorly presented that there was no disguising what it was.

However, in the 70s, wigs were much better and looked so

natural that even women with a good head of hair would wear them. This was a great relief for Mum and from then on, she happily wore a wig.

The newspaper was interested and arranged a time to call and interview Mum. They asked if she would mind if they took a photo of her and she said that would be OK. Before the photographer arrived, I noticed she was not wearing her wig and knowing she would never allow anyone to see her without it, I went to get it for her. She said she did not want to wear it. I could not believe it and said, "But Mum! They want a photo of you, and you said they could have one."

"That is OK, they can take my photo as I am. I don't mind," she said. Mum never wore her wig again and she never wore her earrings or make-up either and she looked beautiful. I now saw an elderly, white-haired lady with lovely skin, high cheekbones and beautiful blue eyes, and her hair was not as sparse as it once was. She was a beauty when she was young, and my mother was beautiful in her old age.

I stayed for ten months. Mum wanted me to go back to Australia to the lovely sunshine and my friends. She was insistent. She always wanted the best for her children; regardless of the hardship it would cause her and Dad. That is why both Mum and Dad encouraged two of their sons to seek a new life with their families in New Zealand. It had been wonderful to be with Mum, play Scrabble, cook nice meals, sing songs, and talk about old times and I was sad to leave her. I knew she could not look after herself as she used to do but she was showered and dressed by home help and she had a cleaner but I also knew that without

Dad and the friends she once had, her life was not very happy.

I tried to take her to see some of the homes that were available for the elderly, as I thought she would be better off, but no! There was no way she was going to leave her home. So, at her repeated request, and because I missed my friends and the sunshine, I returned to Australia. Mum had carefully saved some money from her pension so that I could visit her again. She knew I was now living on a pension and was not as well off as I once was. Knowing time was short, I made sure her money was used as she had intended.

So, I returned to be with her seven months later, having rented a place and made a new home back in Australia.

I knew I would not travel to see her again. I was seventy-five and the journey from Australia was now getting too much for me and I knew Mum would not last much longer. I told her I would not come back when she died. I believed it was more important to be around when she was alive, and we could spend time together.

Spending money to attend a funeral so far away was not something I would consider, and she felt the same. Mum died in December 2001. She was ninety-five. My brother told me she stopped taking her medication two weeks before she died. I know how she felt as I was with her when her doctor told her she was anaemic and had to go into hospital for a blood transfusion. She told her doctor, "Is it to make me live longer, Doctor? Well, I don't want it. Give the blood to a young person who needs it." I understood and I think her doctor did too.

Mum had had enough.

It was a great relief to know that her wonderful spirit and her great courage that I had been privileged to witness were with her until the end. I know it was a happy release for Mum when she died. For me, it was one of the saddest days of my life.

There is no doubt my Mum was special, and I loved her. I miss her more than I ever imagined and not a day passes when I don't think of her and wish she was here.

P.S. I have seen enough of my poor Mum living without the dignity she held so dear and I am now eighty-seven and like many older people I am a member of Exit International. This is an association that believes in voluntary euthanasia and is fighting for government recognition so that we have a choice in the way we die.

It is our hope that many elderly people and those suffering with no hope of getting well can have the choice to leave this world with dignity.

My Dad

Violet Harrington

February 2024

It is twenty-three years since I wrote a story about my mum, and it is only now that I ask myself why I have taken so long to write about my dad?

I am now ninety-seven years of age, and I am writing the words I should have spoken to dad, which sadly I never did. So here I am sharing stories of my dad with you, the reader, so you know the sort of man he was.

I was born a year after Mum and Dad married. Mum was twenty when I was born and three years later my brother Harry came along. Then came Don and when I was seven Derek arrived. By the time Mum was twenty-seven and dad twenty-eight they had four children.

Dad was a master builder and decorator, and it was only after his passing that I realised what a true artist he was. I feel sad that I never told him how much I admired his work, but I am sure he would be comforted to know that his talent has been passed on to me and my eldest son as we are both artists.

I was often with him when he was working, watching the beautiful marbling, graining and gold leaf work he did. He could transform a painted wooden fire surround so that it looked like marble. With the light touch of a feather, he would paint swirls using colours he had mixed himself. There was no *Dulux* in those days. His graining was so perfect that people admired the front door of our house. Knots in the wood and the metal combs he used would change a plain painted door into lovely oak. He was so clever he even made his own stencils, cutting out patterns he designed himself.

My Dad

There was a time when we lived in Dagenham. It was during the Depression and life was hard for Mum and Dad. I was seven and Derek, the youngest, had been born. My dad had outlined panels on my bedroom walls with a basket of flowers painted in the centre. How wonderful and clever he was and yet I took it all for granted, never telling him how much pleasure my bedroom gave me.

Dad loved telling jokes and watching us all laugh. We played indoor games and were very lucky to have young parents as they joined in the fun. Being a family of six it was easy to play games with three each side and Tippet was a favourite.

Some Sundays we would go to hear the Speaker at Hyde Park Corner. Mum and Dad were socialists and as a family we have all grown up with the same political views and kept true to the values we were brought up with. They were atheists and yet every night we would kiss them on the cheek and say, "Good Night, God Bless!" We did that even when we were grown up.

Regent's Park Zoo was another special treat, but I think we only went there once.

Mum and Dad would take us out for the day on a Sunday; they joined in playing cricket and rounders and sometimes we would have a picnic in Greenwich Park. Mum would look very smart with matching clothes and accessories and always wore high heeled shoes. Dad would look good in his suit with matching Tootal tie and pocket handkerchief. They were both tall, presented themselves well and dressed in good taste, wearing the latest fashion.

We often went to Southend on the train to spend a day at the seaside. I was also dressed up in a frilly dress and have a photo of me standing in the sea and that is how it was in those days we dressed for the occasion and not for comfort.

Dad was a quiet man and self-educated. He had to leave school at twelve to look after his mother. I heard over the years that Grandma suffered bilious attacks for years and for which there seemed no reason or remedy.

Mum confessed to being a bit of a bully at school, and she was different from Dad. If she thought you deserved it, she would suddenly lash out with a good hiding as she would call it.

I remember her once saying to Dad, "Talk to the boys Harry, they have been playing up today" and Dad replying, "Hello boys!"

If Mum was ill Dad would look after her and we children were better cared for. Dad would lay the table nicely whereas Mum would put all the knives and forks in the centre of the table, and you helped yourself. Dad would cut out paper and make doyleys for a nice tray to take food to Mum when she was ill.

Dad liked to surprise us and do magic tricks which I believed were truly wonderful. He would say, "Pick a card" and when Dad said, "Hi Di Ho" and pointed somewhere in the room and the card appeared we would be so excited not knowing till years later that Mum had a pack of cards as well. I grew up believing in Father Christmas, fairies, and magic. My parents encouraged this as one year I went into my bedroom and saw a doll's pram. I rushed downstairs to tell Mum and Dad. They listened, glanced at each other and a few minutes later Mum took me back up to my room and to my amazement, the doll's pram had gone. Mum explained that sometimes children are given a vision of what they are getting for Christmas so when I got the pram on Christmas Day, I believed I had the power to see a vision and when a small plane was seen in the sky Mum told me that was Father Christmas on his way home. I ran out in the street waving to the plane and calling out "Thank you Father Christmas!"

We had lovely Christmas games and jokes played on us. A smack in the face with a wet towel after kissing Tutankhamun's face when it was Dad, covered and lying the wrong way so his feet were placed where his face was supposed to be. What fun!

Dad once took a sheet and pinned it to the open door of the living room, leaving an open area top and bottom. With Derek who was a baby on his shoulders Dad would act silly, by using his hands to touch Derek's nose and show Dad's big feet at the bottom. Dad would have been about twenty-nine at that time and looking back I feel so lucky to have had a dad who would do so much to make his children laugh.

I remember a joke dad would tell slowly and quietly. "Who Stole My Golden Arm?" And then after a few minutes of hushed tones he would point and shout, "You Did". Everyone would almost jump out of their skin! In later years my cousins who once stayed with us told me that Dad frightened them when he told them that story.

My brother Derek has told me that if he had been naughty, he would have preferred Dad to spank him rather than talk to him as dad's talk made him feel worse.

That was my dad! Very clever with his use of words. I never knew how it came about but he entered a John Bull Xmas competition and Dad sent in the words

"Aisle, Altar, Hymn" and won a big Xmas hamper as the prize.

He used to joke! "I don't want to hear any of those four-letter words spoken here. Do you understand? Don't say the word WORK!"

When I passed for Grammar School, I had to wear the uniform and I would need a satchel and tools. It was never discussed how much it would all cost and although Dad had a gambling problem, we never went short and whenever he had a big win on the dogs, he would spend it on the family.

In later years I learned that a cousin also passed for Grammar School but sadly her parents could not afford for her to go. However she married and lived on The Isle of Wight, where she was able to use her gift as an artist. Owners of boats would commission her to paint pictures of their boats and so she earned money and fulfilled her artistic talent.

We could bring friends home any time and they would always be welcomed. If we were going to have a meal it would be shared. No problem! One school friend told me she liked having tea with us as we had best butter whereas she had margarine at home.

Dad always wrote beautiful words on the birthday cards he bought for mum and despite all their quarrels I knew he loved her. We were brought up to respect our parents and dad always showed Mum respect but sadly their quarrels were too much and too often. Not good for me when I went to bed not knowing whether I was going to live with mum and if my three younger brothers would go with Dad. This is how they would end their rows.

But all would be well the next morning with them acting as if there had not been a cross word between them the night before. I was too young to understand how couples can make up their differences in bed.

So, they lived that way all through their married life. Quarrelling, talking about divorce, and then making up.

My Paternal Grandparents

My grandad Hugh was also a master builder and decorator and owned an antique shop. His wife had died when their daughter Rosie was a little girl. He met and married my grandma Martha who was a war widow, and she had a little girl called Edie. Dad was their first born and so he grew up with two stepsisters. Later came Alice, then Fred, then Robert and then Lillian.

There was a tradition that the eldest sons were called Hugh Henry and then the next one would be Henry Hugh. My dad was Henry Hugh and my brother Hugh Henry, and all were called Harry. Crazy! I think of Christmas and remember so well how Grandma and Grandad would come on Christmas eve just before we children went to bed. We would hear them chatting and having a drink with Mum and Dad and it was music to our ears.

Next morning we would receive our presents from them. It was the same for many years.

For my brother's chocolate cigarettes and cigars, and a small handbag for me with sixpences inside. I loved it when we went to see my dad's parents. It was not often but it was always on a Sunday.

Granddad had a Dalmatian dog called Floss and they had such beautiful antique ornaments and paintings which I admired and now know how valuable they must have been. A very large Jacobean sideboard had lots of goodies laid out on it for us to eat. I think Grandma made toffee called 'Stick Jaw' specially for the children. It was good to see mum and dad laugh and dad debate politics with the uncles and mum would chat with the aunts, and my brothers and I would play games with our cousins. That's what people did before TV!

The story I heard was that granddad was a Dr Barnardo's boy and a Lay Preacher at one time. In those days you never questioned to find out more which is sad as I would have liked to know more about my lovely granddad.

It would be dark and late at night when we got home, and dad would have Derek on his shoulders as we walked from the bus stop. Happy memories!

The War

The skies were bright red, bombs were falling, and you could hear the overhead hum of German planes as they dropped their bombs. It was frightening when the siren sounded, and we had to leave our cosy beds and run to the air raid shelter. The next morning, we would find whole streets demolished by land mines and hear of people we knew who had died.

Regardless of his work dad made up his mind: we had to leave as it was too dangerous. We all went to see dad's mum and dad to ask them to leave with us, but they said no, they could not leave the family.

So, we left with just suitcases.

Dad was in charge and oversaw mum's sisters and their children, mum's mum, and all of us. We became evacuees and moved to Reading where dad and mum lived for the rest of their days.

So, Dad's family stayed in London all through the bombing, sleeping every night in the underground for shelter. All were safe when the war ended, and we were able to see them. I look back to those days now and realise Dad had none of his close family with him and Mum had most of hers and so she was happy especially as Dad was now assigned to war work and there was no more dog racing.

Now back to my dad

He was a handsome young man but when he was twenty-two, he developed an abscess on his neck. The doctor gave him something to rub on it, but it got worse, was very swollen and painful. He had to go to The London Hospital, where they lanced it. By mistake, in so doing, they cut the facial nerves, leaving dad with one side of his face drooping and paralysed.

I was used to seeing Dad this way, but people used to stare at him; I know he was very conscious of how he looked.

It was sad to see Dad looking in the mirror taking out some grit that had got in his eye as he could not close one eye.

I never knew Dad bothered about the way he looked until he was about sixty.

He told me that he had read in the papers about an operation that was being performed to paralyse the 'good' side of the face and so make it look the same.

He said he wanted to have the chance of the operation. Both mum and I were horrified at the idea and told him that we never noticed his face was different and we did not want him to change. He never talked about it again.

My poor dad! How sad he must have been all those years! Maybe that is why he never socialized. Of course, now in these days he would have received compensation for such medical negligence.

It is now many years later and we have all married and moved miles away. I lived in West Yorkshire for twenty years. My three children would visit Mum and Dad when they could, but they did not live near them.

Harry my brother who was born when I was three, lived in Maidenhead not far from Mum and Dad. He and his wife and four daughters would be around for them which was a great relief.

Mum and Dad were now in their eighties.

At that time, Donald and Derek had moved to New Zealand with their wives and children. Much later I also went to live in New Zealand. I realise now how sad it must have been for them not to have their children nearby and how Mum and Dad missed out on having a family around them. Regardless of how they felt they always put us children first and they encouraged us all to live better lives.

One year I came back to England as Don told me that Dad was in hospital. Don and Derek had been back to see Mum and Dad during these years and Mum and Dad had been to New Zealand and spent six months with the family.

Mum opened the door, she was so weak, leaning up against the wall and worn out from walking to catch the bus to the hospital to see Dad each day.

I hired a car and went with her to the hospital. Dad was in bed very thin, and he cried and said he wanted to be home with Mum. I asked the nurse, and she said I had to see the specialist as Dad was not supposed to leave the hospital. So, I arranged to speak to the Psychiatrist who was treating him. I was surprised as I never saw Dad as a mental patient. She told me that Dad had been admitted with the express orders he was never to go back to that house where he was locked in the room and never fed.

This was news to me as Mum was known for years to give Dad big meals he could not eat and as for locking dad in a room that was unheard of. I asked the doctor what the diagnosis for Dad was when he was admitted. She said malnutrition.

Having been married to a psychiatrist for twenty-seven years I had learned a lot and I said, "You know that malnutrition brings on hallucinations and my mother would never lock Dad in a room or not feed him". I explained to the doctor that they really wanted to be together, and Dad was so unhappy. I told her they had a love-hate relationship all their married lives and could not live without each other. Thankfully I was able to convince her, and she understood, and agreed that Dad could come home.

He was so happy, so was Mum and so was I.

I made the front room into a bedroom and bought heavy velvet curtains as Mum was not happy as she said people could see in the room of a night when the light was on.

I bought a baby alarm so Mum could hear if Dad needed her in the night and as she was burning the toast under the gas grill, I bought an electric toaster. I also bought a bedside table for Dad and when the bed was delivered, I got the chap to take the settee away to make room. Mum never knew he charged me to remove it as she had imagined they would pay her something for it. It was such a joy to see Dad comfortable and Mum with him. They were so devoted and could not be happy unless they were together.

Once home I got in touch with their GP who had not been looking after them properly as he was supposed to see them every year but had not. I decided to make a complaint. I had an appointment for the Monday but before that could happen the doctor went to see them and arranged for a social worker to come and a Health Visitor who arranged Meals on Wheels and anything else they needed. Mum could not believe the help that was available. She told me later that she stopped the Meals on Wheels as they did not like them. Also she turned off the baby alarm as she heard every sound Dad made and so she could not sleep.

So, I stayed for a while before visiting my children and friends. It was a lovely time to be with them and see them happy and settled before I returned to New Zealand.

Dad died two years later. He was eighty-six and Mum lived on till 2002 when she was ninety-five. She missed dad so much and I know she never enjoyed life after he had gone.

I never went to his funeral but went to the cemetery on my next visit and saw the tree that was planted with his name.

Cheryl took me as her mother was buried in the same cemetery and we planted loads of daffodil bulbs round dad's tree.

I sent this story to my daughter-in-law Liz, and I am copying her reply to show that at seventy Dad was still making magic for little children.

"Just thought you'd like to have a memory of mine of your dad from when Manfred and Gabriel and I visited. Gabe would be about three and your dad pointed up at an airplane flying over and whilst Gabriel was looking up, he dropped some sweets on the floor saying, 'Oh look what the airplane has dropped'. I thought both your mum and dad very friendly, homely, and welcoming."

It is important to know that Gabe was their first great grandchild and Manfred was my first born.

I end this story hoping I have managed to show something about Dad that made him special. For his children, grandchildren, and great grandchildren he left fond memories to cherish. Just one last thing about dad before I close:

He made lovely toffee apples.

Lots of love Dad wherever you are.

Vi xxx

Written on the 1st of March 2024.

Choices!

Lorraine Roxon

As one grows older and there is not much to look forward to, one tends to look back to the past.

So many women look at photos of when they were young and cannot believe how attractive they were. But it is not only women; it's the same for men. Most would agree that when they were young they were completely unaware of their looks.

Technology today offers the opportunity for so many people to find out about their family histories and they go looking into the past. Old photos turn up and you hear families say, "Look at Grandma! Wasn't she beautiful!" and "Look at Grandad! Wasn't he handsome?"

I feel safe in saying I doubt very much if they saw themselves as beautiful or handsome.

Many years ago, I knew a woman who baby sat for me. She was about fifty five and told me she had been a model when younger. I looked at her; she was overweight and did not look attractive. I thought, "She was never a model!" Now I can see I must have been wrong.

It is the year 2014 and as I write this I am eighty-seven years of age. My skin is wrinkled, my hair is grey, my eyes have lost their shine and my hands show signs of arthritis, but fortunately my brain is still very active. Looking back now I have come to realise the opportunities offered to me years ago could only have come about because of my appearance. For many who never knew me reading about these missed opportunities might be hard to accept, but I am sure I am not alone and many will read this and see similarities which they can relate to. Many like me, will find themselves questioning what would their lives be now, if they had taken a different path.

I was intelligent and artistic as a child but I was very self conscious about my appearance as I had a fold of skin in the corner of my eyes which made my eyes look slanted. There was no doubt I looked different and I was bullied at school and called "Chinese Eyes'. This would not happen today with so many people of different nationalities attending our schools. (Although I stand corrected as I understand my grandson Asher was also called 'Chinese Eyes' at primary and secondary school. He is now seventeen, considered by many as very handsome and often referred to as the Korean lad!).

I was about eight at the time when I came home from school crying. Mum was not home. She was with her friend Miss Minnie next door. I ran next door crying.

"They are picking on me again ... calling me Chinese Eyes".

Miss Minnie said, "Why are you so upset? You have lovely blue eyes and you will know this when you are older." Of course I knew she would have to say something like that and it did nothing to make me feel better.

It was hard on my mother to have a snivelling daughter who could not stand up for herself. "Hit them back if they hit you!" she would say but I would cry and say "I was not born to fight."

Mum admitted that she had been the school bully but as long as she could recite the Catechism the nuns thought she was the perfect pupil. On finding out that I was taking a detour to avoid the school bullies, she gave me this ultimatum: "I am telling you now", she said, "If you don't come home the normal way from school tomorrow, it will be me who will give you a good hiding but if you do I will give you sixpence." That was my Mum!

I walked the short way home and passed the group of girls. They let me pass without incident. I got the sixpence as Mum promised and I was not bothered any more. They still called after me but they never got close and pushed me as they had before.

I am sad to say my mother did make me conscious of the fact that I was plain as she had my hair permed when I was eleven so I looked better. "Why do you smile with your mouth closed?" she would say. "Show your teeth, stand up straight, stop stooping". I knew she meant well but it made me feel even more self conscious. Mum was tall, good looking and very fashionable. I was so proud of her whenever she came to my school.

I know I caused her great embarrassment when it was the Jubilee Party. I was about ten then and the street organised a stage where people would entertain. Mum told me she had put my name down to go on the stage and sing and tap dance. It was not surprising Mum would do this as I used to entertain the local kids in the street. I went up on the stage and I could hardly speak. My voice was so quiet and I did a quick tap dance and ran off the stage and hid. When Mum finally found me she was upset and told me, "You made me look such a fool" and I knew she was right.

Poor Mum! I can see how I let her down and how she had high hopes for me even then. I was twelve and a half when the war started.

London was considered safe. The Barrage Balloons that encircled London were seen as impenetrable and no German planes would be able get through. Sirens would sound but soon the "All Clear" would be heard. It was a warning that

German planes had been seen leaving France but had not reached London. I would watch from my upstairs bedroom window and see the guns on the Mudchute move upwards to the sky and turn in different directions but no German planes would be seen.

We were used to the sirens sounding of a night and leaving our warm beds to go down to the shelter in the garden and then the "All Clear" would sound and back to our beds we would go.

However this pattern did not last long before the German planes got through the barrage balloons.

The drone of the German planes flying over us of a night was very frightening. Whole streets were being demolished and people were dead and dying. It was not long before Mum and Dad decided we had to leave. So our family with some of Mum's family left 'The Island'. There were many cities being bombed, not just London, and many families left their homes to live in safer areas. We were known as 'evacuees' and we left London to live in Reading.

This move was not of choice but like many it was one we were forced to make. We were all upset, especially as we could not find our cat Ginger but Dad went back and found her and so all was well in the end.

As for my education, I had missed too many lessons and had fallen behind to the point it was impossible for me to catch up even though I had been such a good pupil before the war.

I asked Mum and Dad if I could leave school and go to work and I felt a great sense of relief when they agreed although at the time I was not really ready to grow up. I was wearing socks, flat heeled shoes and school uniform and I still enjoyed playing Cowboys and Indians with my three younger brothers. But once I went to work the change in me was instantaneous. I became very fashion conscious and was able to style my long hair in the latest fashions. I loved using lipstick and seeing the difference in my appearance and I wore shoes with a Cuban heel and stockings. I was lucky to have good skin; my hair was a chestnut colour and shiny. I was told I looked like the film stars of that time Gene Tierney and then Ava Gardner and in later years, Sophia Loren. They were all beautiful women but although these observations were flattering, they did nothing for me.

Mum made sure I never took any notice of compliments and told me, "When you are married you must make up as soon as you get up in the morning, as you look awful without any on."

Dad on the other hand had taken the trouble to tell me that beauty came from within and not from outside. My poor dad, a handsome man of twenty-two had suffered with a facial paralysis that happened when he had an infection in his neck. The London Hospital operated and had cut some vital nerves. Dad was told there was nothing they could do as the infection was so bad he would have died. I felt so sad as people would stare at him and I knew he was embarrassed.

I started work and did well in my office job at Allied Suppliers as I was good at figures. Many of the large firms had moved from London and had their offices in Reading. It was not long before I left that job as Mum had seen the 'Wanted Cashier and Bookkeeper' notice in the window of a large gown shop in Broad Street, Reading's town centre.

"You can do that," she said, "and it will be more money". So I applied and got the position and Mum was right. It was a better salary. Mum always wanted the best for me and made me feel I could do anything I set my mind to or maybe on reflection could it be what she set her mind to?

It was war time and the lifestyle for single young women if not in the forces was to work, go home, have a meal, dress up and go out and join their friends at the local dance hall. There were plenty of offers from soldiers stationed in the area to walk a girl home after a dance. "Just walk me home. Nothing at the end of it," I would warn them and most would accept this although a date for the next evening was the usual ending. That would sometimes mean future dates and meeting Mum, Dad and my brothers.

I had to be home at 11.00 pm at the latest; in those days that was the accepted rule for girls. It gave us enough time to enjoy ourselves, get home, have sufficient sleep and be up for work next morning. The idea of today's clubs where kids go at 11.00 pm and stay till 3.00am is beyond my comprehension.

The lifestyle then was to go for walks, to the pictures, dancing and joining in the family events. Due to the war situation it was recognised that a serviceman could easily feel the need to ask a girl to have a more serious relationship and get married. Many were far too young and chose to. I was one who chose not to.

There was always the knowledge of the young man being moved on and you would never see them again. The request, "Will you write to me?" always received a spontaneous, "Yes! Of course I will". You would write but for how long one never knew. I was writing to five young servicemen at one point. It was war time and a letter meant a lot; we were all conscious of the fact they might never return.

Although I had quite a few boy-friends I was still very self conscious about the way I looked. I used to stare in the mirror and look closely at my eyes and think, if only I could cut the fold of skin I am sure my eyes would open up and I would look better. Not so strange to think this way when some Chinese girls are choosing to have this done today by cosmetic surgeons.

The years pass and the war is over at last. I am now eighteen and a half, tall, slim and due to the many compliments I knew I was seen as attractive. Also I wore clothes that were different.

I had always loved clothes, having drawn pictures and designs when a school girl. I wanted to be a fashion designer and once I started work I was allowed to design some of my own clothes. Mum was very kind and encouraged this flair. She took me to the shops, letting me choose materials which she bought. A local dressmaker then made up my designs.

Life was slowly getting back to normal and a Victorian Ball was to be held at the Reading Town Hall. My mother encouraged me to go and a friend's mother who had acted in the play, "The Importance of Being Ernest", had a beautiful black and white striped gown with a boned bodice. It was in the Victorian style and she loaned it to me. I did my hair and make-up and felt very glamorous. It was all so exciting! Mum arranged for a taxi to take me to the ball and I won first prize! Mum was so thrilled when I got home and told her.

As I write, I feel sad as I realise how much Mum must have

missed out in her young life. Having married at eighteen and with four children by the age of twenty seven she must have loved sharing in my excitement.

It was a few months later when Mum read an article in the newspaper about Lucy Clayton and her modelling school in London.

"We must phone and make an appointment," she said.

I knew Mum had been told when she was a young woman that she should have been a mannequin and I am sure she could have been but I did not feel it was for me. Parading up and down with people watching me did not appeal at all but the prospect of wearing lovely clothes was a great attraction.

Anyway we went to London both full of anticipation of what the future might hold. I was interviewed and made to feel very special as I was told I had everything needed to make a perfect mannequin. We left the office and I remember a pub nearby with the sound of a piano and the music "Summer Time". For many years Mum and I spoke of the memories this song evoked in us.

It was all very well being accepted, but now we had to think of where I would stay. In those days and with my upbringing there was no way I would be allowed to share a flat. It had to be with a family and so it was arranged that I live with my elderly childless aunt and uncle. They lived in Bush Hill Park, Enfield and they had always liked me and said they would love to have me live with them.

The fact I would leave my parents and my brothers who were young and full of fun was never given any thought. I had started a new life and the world was my oyster. Not that I wanted my life to change but I was nineteen and it was time to move on. I would catch the steam train to Liverpool Street station and then go by tube to Oxford Street. I did this five days a week and after six weeks I passed the diploma course at Lucy Clayton's with an 'A'.

My tutor was upset with me. She said, "I told the judges, this girl uses her hands so well and you let me down as you never did". I was sorry that she felt let down but I was nervous at the time and anyway I was graded "A" and that was enough.

After we graduated we were given a list of possible jobs and I had ticked the boxes. No! I would not model lingerie. No! I would not model swimwear. Such was my attitude although looking back I think I was stupid as I am sure my mother would have told me to tick "Yes!"

Once we graduated the office would send us to interviews seeking employment. My first interview was at Jays in Oxford Street. This was a large well respected store of quality. The showroom was at the top of the store. It covered a large area and was beautifully furnished. I was nervous and did my walk and my twirl for the man who was going to decide whether to employ me.

He asked me, "Where do you come from?"

"Reading."

"No! Before that."

"London."

"No! Before that."

I did not know what more he wanted and he then said: "I thought you were Javanese". I had never heard of Java but it was enough to add to my confusion as to my looks.

I was offered the position but declined. The salary was not good enough. Back at Lucy's the girls said, "You are mad!" They pointed out opportunities that came from such a position which made no impression on me at all.

One day I was walking down the stairs when Lucy Clayton was passing. She stopped me and said, "Have you been sent for an audition for the film London Town?" I said that I had not. She took my arm and we went straight back to the reception desk. She asked, "Why has this girl not been sent to audition for the London Town film?" The receptionist replied, "They want girls who look English Lucy and she doesn't." A long pause, she looked at me and agreed. "Oh yes. I see." So with that, she apologised and left.

I was then sent to model for a fur coat store but I did not look sophisticated enough they said, so I never got that job.

At one interview the receptionist told me that Violet was not a name for a model and suggested I call myself Lorraine which is what I did from that time on.

Soon after that I was sent to audition at the Prince of Wales Theatre. It was for a show girl at Tom Arnold's show at Blackpool Opera House. I went because it was arranged for me and not by choice. I was not feeling nervous and did so well they sent me a letter offering me the position and I replied politely refusing it.

I knew I would love wearing the clothes but being on stage and being watched by so many was not for me.

My aunt and uncle and my mother were so annoyed with me. "How could you refuse such a wonderful opportunity? Live life with a capital L!" my mother said. Looking back now I can understand how Mum felt. My mother spoke about it years later when talking to a friend about the opportunities I had missed.

"You know what she told me?" mum said to her friend. "She wanted to be married and have children".

It was true! I never wanted to be a model or have a position which could bring me fame or fortune. I wanted to feel secure. I wanted children and a husband and to be a good mother and a faithful wife.

Little did my family know how afraid I was of going into the world of show business. I was not worldly wise. I was very naïve and gullible and I was aware of this. The stories I had heard of the way girls became successful was frightening.

During this time I went out with a man I met through a group of friends. He was older and the friends told me he was a nice man and I should go out with him So I agreed to see a film with him.

He was polite and he told me he was so pleased to see I had a small scar on my forehead as it would be too much to have such unblemished beauty. Such crazy talk! I went to dinner with him but I found his conversation dull and as I was not interested in seeing him again, I told him so. He knew the photographer who worked for 'Lilliput'. This was a well known small booklet style magazine and he wanted me to meet his friend. "He will put your photo in the magazine" he told me and I replied that I was not interested. I saw him three times — once with my friends and that was enough. A week after I told him I did not want to see him again I got a shock as I found him walking behind me after I had left the train and was almost home. He must have caught the train when he saw me get on it. I ran in the house and my Uncle went out and told him he would inform the police if he followed me again. I was nervous but thankfully he never bothered me again. He was completely infatuated with me so the friends told me and I was glad I had the sense not to encourage him.

During this time I finally took work as a house model to a firm in Wells Street. This was in the area I knew well as it was a side road off Oxford Street and near Lucy's school. It was while working there I missed an opportunity I never told Mum about. I was at Bourne and Hollingsworth's which was across the road from where I worked. A few of us met almost every day for lunch there. On this day a man who was also lunching kept looking at me. As he left he came up to me and gave me his card and asked if I would go to his office the next day and could I make it for 1.00 pm. I looked at his card and it had his name and the address Wardour Street, Film Agent. I said I would be there. My lunch pals were all excited and one offered to come with me. So we went, even though I was not that keen. We arrived at 12.55 and were told we would not be kept long. We waited and at 1.15 pm I said, "I am not waiting any longer. Let's go!" and we left. I think Mum would have really been annoyed if she had known about that opportunity.

I was happy with my job as it was a manufacturing firm and the people who worked there were very kind. There were four bosses and the chief boss Mr Rosenbaum was a very sick man suffering with cancer. He had fled Vienna before the Nazis came. Sometimes I would be taken to his home to model an outfit from the new line so he could make his views known. There was a problem for the five men on the sales team. The firm had not yet received the materials and the sample dresses had not been made. The team were due to go on the road shortly and there was a great deal of concern.

I had an idea and used the drawing of a standard model and drew pictures of each of the dresses as they would look when made. I even showed the saddle stitching if it was part of the design. We clipped swatches of the materials to be used to the drawings and these drawings were used by the salesmen to go on the road and get their orders. Mr Rosenbaum was so impressed that he offered to pay for me to go to Brook Street Art College. I would have loved to go to Brook Street but they had no part time courses and so I could not go and so it was out of the question.

Now that is really what I would class as a missed opportunity. I would have been doing what I really wanted to do.

The company dealt only with stores with a good reputation and I modelled for the individual buyers of these stores. I got to know the buyers of the London Stores well and when their store put on a fashion show for an evening event they would offer me work and so I would earn extra money. I refused Luncheon shows as I would not model when people were eating. Maybe I was wrong but I saw it as disrespectful and I only worked when there was a cat walk. Sadly we never had music as they do today and that would have made modelling so much easier and enjoyable than having a woman commentator.

Our designer Madame Simone was French and my dresses,

suits and evening gowns had to be made to fit me as I was not a standard size. My hips were 36 when they should have been 38. I can remember the pain when a pin scratched all the way down my arm when I was taking off the dress and once I fainted when I had to stand for a long time while being fitted. I was wearing a winter suit when it was very hot weather. We were a firm of wholesalers and clothes were shown and sold for the forthcoming season. So I modelled summer clothes in the winter and winter clothes in the summer. Madame Simone's son, a nice young man on leave, invited me to The Chelsea Arts Ball but I had heard stories about what went on at the Ball so I declined. Pity as I might have had a good time. It is no surprise when I look back that people looked at me. I wore the very latest fashion which was Dior when I went to see my family in Reading. As you can imagine my brothers were all proud of their sister and Derek the youngest still speaks of the time when we went to the films and an advert came up on the screen showing a coat in the latest fashion. I remember it was a *Windsmoor* coat with two cape sleeves and I was wearing it. When the lights went up and we were leaving the cinema it was only natural that people would look at me having seen the coat on the screen.

One day I was very excited as I heard one of the bosses was going to a fashion show in Paris and there was talk that I was going as well. The manageress who was thirty-five and single, said, "You know if you go to Paris what will be expected of you?" I expect I will have to model some clothes," I said. She soon put me right: "The boss will expect you to sleep with him."

"Oh no!" I said totally shocked at such an idea. "You are wrong. I am sure the boss would not expect that of me."

"Don't be so naïve," she said. "I went to Paris and that is what happened to me." She told me she didn't mind and it is better sex than when you are married. I replied, "How can you know that when you have never been married?"

Stella was wrong. My bosses knew me well enough and I was not asked to go to Paris. One of the bosses did grab me once and kiss me and I made it very clear that I was annoyed. He got the message and was always kind and polite and never tried again. He did bring me back a gift from the trip to Paris. It was a *Waspie* which was being worn at the time. It was a boned bodice which made the waist smaller and was right for the 'New Look' (as the Dior fashion was called).

Some eyebrows were raised when he gave me the gift but I knew there was no ulterior motive and the words, "Thank You" would be more than enough. I was right.

One day I was at the Tate Gallery exhibition of Van Gogh with David, (the man I later married), when I was approached by a very distinguished looking man with a goatee beard and a very well dressed lady who was with him.

He said, "I am an RA and I wonder if you would consider allowing me to make a bust of you as I plan to exhibit this year." I was flattered and gave him my phone number. My fiancé did not like the idea and so I never sat. He phoned many times but I told him I was too busy and in the end to please my fiancé who was very possessive, I said, "Sorry! I can't make it."

When I told my aunt and uncle, my uncle said, "I would have been so proud if your aunt had such an opportunity," and he was very upset that I had let such an opportunity pass. I knew he was right but I considered David's feelings.

I end my story hoping whoever reads it finds it interesting and can relate to it and will agree that ...

Lost opportunities mean nothing if you achieve that which is most important to you and makes you happy.

I was fortunate to have a husband, and three lovely children, nine grandchildren and two great grandchildren and time to be involved in Fund Raising for Charities.

Illustration 2: Photo taken 1990. Left to right: Manfred, Yolanda and Gordon with Yolanda's two children, Miriam and Reuben

I married David when I was twenty two. He was a doctor, fourteen years older than me and I was able to be the wife and mother I wanted to be.

Illustration 3: David and me July 16th 1949

A Golden Oldie in Cyber Space.

Lorraine Roxon

Illustration 4: *Cy and Lorraine with her first Computer.*

It is the year nineteen ninety-seven and like so many people at that time we had accumulated all the electric gadgets that are supposed to make life easier and save time. There was the blender, a crêpe machine, the sandwich maker, the electric crock pot, the machine to make froth on the coffee, and let's not forget, the electric can opener which could open one hundred cans in a minute (so it said on the instruction sheet).

Now I ask you, we are just two people, so when would we ever need to open so many cans at once? I believed at the time all these gadgets would help us to save time and that would make our life easier.

However, it was not long before the electric can opener was shut away in the cupboard with many other 'Make life easier Gadgets', and the old hand operated can opener was dug out from the old box in the garage and returned to its rightful place in the kitchen drawer.

I was constantly asking my husband to buy the new products the television and newspapers advertised as they really sounded good.

Now who could resist the latest CD player? The one that plays five CDs at a time. We would be able to have hours of continuous music, and of our choice. Now wouldn't that be wonderful? Well, we did buy one and it was great—for a while—till I found I was too busy or too lazy to change the discs and the same music was heard, repeatedly.

Like many seniors we decided to sell out large house and we moved into a smaller house with a small garden and less housework. However due to having a smaller kitchen and less cupboard space our electrical appliances and our pots and pans took up too much room. Cupboards were bulging, and labour-saving kitchen devices were in cupboards situated low down. They were too big to leave on the top of the kitchen bench. Some were too tall and too heavy to go on to higher shelves. That meant we had to put them in cupboards low down. So, we were obliged to bend down to get them and lift them up to use them. We were of an age when all this was too much and we found it was easier to use a fork for whisking, and the old-fashioned potato masher which required no effort.

One day, we decided we would be ruthless and make more room. Our time-saving gadgets just had to go. I discovered that my husband did not like froth on his coffee and I did not like the crepes the machine made and that was the reason why those gadgets had not been used for years. So, we sold some for next to nothing at a garage sale. Some had stopped working ages ago and had been waiting to be repaired. They were taking up valuable space and were not worth the cost of repair, so out they went. We tried hard to give away things that were working and almost new and in good order. We were sure they would be gratefully received, but to our surprise no one wanted them. "We had a job to give them away" our friends told us So they went to the 'Salvos', and we decided from then on we would not buy any more gadgets. No more spending money on gadgets which were supposed to save us time and so make our lives easier.

As we were retired, we had more time for many things which we could not do before. Added to which, our appetites were smaller, so it took less time to cook, and we used less utensils. We also had to be careful how we spent our money.

So, who in their right mind, retired and watching their expenses would contemplate buying a computer—even though we were bombarded by adverts telling us how important it was to buy one? That would be the last thing we would need and anyway they cost a lot.

So, Hooray! Here was a new gadget which left me cold and with absolutely no desire to own. I just was not interested, and no way was I going to be tempted.

Our friend, Danny, who was an artist, began to expound the wonders of a computer, as he had just finished a course at the 'Tech'. "The prices have come down such a lot now," he said, "Come and see the artwork I am doing and, if you like, I will teach you. I can send you to the place where I bought my computer. They will give you a good deal and look after you. Look, Lorraine, I tell you, it would be great for you, and I know you would get a lot out of it."

Being an artist myself I listened and wondered, and I observed the wonderful things Danny was able to do with his Corel Draw Program, I was fascinated and very impressed. I found using the mouse was hard though and I could not position it easily. I did not think I would ever be able to click the mouse and move things about the screen the way Danny did.

Yes! I had to admit it was all very impressive and intriguing but not for me and I was pleased to see I had finally reached the stage when there was nothing I needed, wanted, or could be tempted to buy.

One day, my husband, Cy, said to me, "You know I think we should buy a computer. You will be able to put your poetry together at last. That would be good for you, and I think you would get a lot out of using a computer". He went on to say, "It would be no good to me. I wouldn't have any idea how to work one, but you have always been good with gadgets, and I think you could do what Danny does. You are an artist and I really think it would be good for you."

This was a surprise as Cy was always trying to stop me from buying things. Mind you! it was as Cy said. I had been writing for many years, but it had been typed on an old typewriter many years ago and was certainly not up to a standard that would allow me to submit my work to a publisher. People who had read my poems liked them, and I was told many times that I should do something about getting them published. Some had been read over the air and so I knew they were acceptable. As for being good with gadgets, it was true. I was the one who mended things and could set things up. Cy did not have that sort of interest and I was very surprised to see how keen he was for me to have a computer.

So, I thought it over carefully. There was no doubt I was impressed, and Danny had offered to help me, So I made up mind and agreed we would go for it and buy a computer.

How many Rams and Megabytes? These words meant nothing to me but I was in Danny's hands now and I felt safe. A fifteen-inch monitor was much better than a fourteen and so we went for the bigger one.

Speakers? Yes, I must have speakers and it will be great to see my poems in print. What sort of a printer do you want?' asked Danny.

A printer? I never thought about that. Silly me! You can't print without a printer. So I bought all my computer ware and I received a package with some free discs. We came home with all the big boxes and it was installed in our spare bedroom. There was already a desk, so it fitted in well.

Danny kindly installed the programs, and I was ecstatic. Many times, I had to phone Danny to come and help me, and so many times I felt I had ruined everything. I was afraid that I would break the computer and worried about the cost involved for the repair.

It slowly became obvious that this silent monster had invaded our home and was slowly taking me over. But not so silently really, for every day when I switched on my computer a wonderful Microsoft jingle would fill my ears. This heralded the time for wondrous things to happen and I would become full of excitement. I had also been surprised to find that I could play my music discs and listen to them while I was working, so that was an extra bonus of which I had been unaware.

By this time, I was reading all I could, buying books and software and marvelling at the wonders I was beginning to perform with my new found companion. As time went on I grew more confident, and I managed to write letters that looked professional, add pictures with colour and my poetry began to take shape.

We bought my computer two months before my 70th birthday and on my birthday my son Gordon sent me the software program Publisher 97.

"You will need this, Mum, if you want to make books of your poetry". He had been so thrilled when I told him I had a computer and suggested that now we should consider going on the Internet so that we could be in touch.

I thrust that thought from my mind, I was not ready to tackle something new and wondered if I ever would be. Danny kindly installed the Publisher Program for me, but after a while he decided that I was getting too confused with so many programs and he deleted it. The idea being to re-install it at a later date. "It is too much for you to learn yet, concentrate on *Word* and when you have learned that you can then think about Publisher".

He was right! I really was getting confused. There was so much for me to learn and I wanted to know everything so quickly. I had this insatiable desire to learn everything I could, and as fast as possible.

Six months later my husband said, "Why don't you get on the Internet? It would be great to be able to be in touch with Gordon and I know you would love that."

At the time, I seemed to have gone off writing and was not using my computer as much. The Internet sounded exciting, and so, here I was again, caught up in the new gadget indoctrination. However, the thought of being in touch with my son so easily and at such little—cost only $1.00 per hour I was told—was something I could not resist. Another expense another gadget, but how wonderful it all was.

I was so excited. To be on the Internet I must have a Modem, I was told. And so another new word I had learned 'Modem'. They were all different prices, and when I was told they were around $75 upwards, I thought this is great, we can afford to buy one without it hurting our pockets too much. However, I discovered that the speed of the modem, (bits per second), was the criteria by which you judged its performance. It would be better if I bought one that was fast, if I wanted to Surf the Net without waiting a long time before getting started.

So, I settled for the latest and fastest which at the time was 33.6

BPS. After all, didn't everything have to be fast? So once again, here I was trying to save time.

'Bits per second' more words which I didn't really understand but I was beginning to feel proud about the new knowledge I had gained.

So Cyber Space here I come!

Now I had to decide which Server I would sign up with. These are the people I would 'buy time' from. Here I was retired and with lots of time, 'Buying Time'. It all sounded crazy, but this was different. This was the time I would use on the Internet. Another friend, already on the Internet, kindly advised me who was the best Server to go to and explained the cost.

I bought a package which gave me four hundred hours to use in one year and no monthly restrictions. This seemed to be the way to go. So, with my modem connected to my Server, and my Server having installed a browser, I was finally ready to Surf the Net. Wow! The mind boggles with so much terminology.

I thought it would be a good idea if I treated myself to a dictionary and learn some of these new words that kept popping up. By this time, I was really becoming very cautious about spending. However I decided that a little book was essential if I wanted to become familiar with this computer language which was so new to me.

Well, don't you believe it! This was no little book. This book was thick and large. The price was more than I had expected, and it contained thousands of words.

I put the book down, walked out of the shop and decided I would never ever need to learn or use so many words. Danny was not on the Internet and so it was up to me to buy books and teach myself. I did a couple of mornings at our local Tech, but that didn't hep as the students were young and already knew so much. I had already built up quite a library with books 'For Dummies' which was a very apt description of me, and now added to my library were new books about The Internet. Again, 'For Dummies' All of them I read avidly and gradually, my whole world was changing.

Every night I would go to bed and read as much as I could take into my brain and then I would feel obliged to get up in the middle of the night and see if what I had learned I could transfer to the screen.

My days began to get very long, and my nights were getting shorter, but I didn't care. It was all so new, so wonderful and so exciting, especially when something new I read and put into practice, worked. Happily, this was happening to me more often and my confidence began to grow.

I was now able to show my husband some of the wonderful places we could visit and learn about. "Look at London. The people are moving on the screen! And it is all happening at this minute as we watch. Isn't it wonderful? And look at Mars, can you imagine, we are looking at it now, where the spacecraft is at this very minute?"

We sat for hours in awe and were amazed at all the exciting things we were able to see and learn about. Yes, this really was wonderful, and we felt pleased that we could enjoy so much. We thought about the cost, but at only $1 for an hour we knew we were getting very good value. This was our new form of entertainment, and we loved it. Forget about television and the cinema, we sat glued for hours at our new screen. Oh dear! Excuse me, not screen it is a 'Monitor'.

However, it was about a month later when I discovered that while we were Surfing the Net, no one could reach us on the phone as we were using the telephone line. No one had told me about this when I went on to the Internet, and then when I asked, I was told that many people had mobile phones and that was the answer. However, I looked into this and thought of all the friends who phone us. They are mostly pensioners like us and they would have to pay more for a call to speak to us on a mobile phone, so that was out. Here we go again, I thought, will it never end? What did I let myself in for? And how many more expenses will I suddenly discover?

So, I had to have a new telephone line, which meant a rental charge for a second line, but at least I was lucky as there was a special offer which was half the usual price for installation, so that made it a bit easier.

At last that was it! Finished! No more extras to pay and now I was able to use the Internet without any worry.

I was due to go to England in October that year to see my family and friends and was to be away for two months I kissed my husband, cuddled our Chow-Chow unplugged and covered my computer and left for England. Two whole months without my husband and two whole months without my computer. However, would I survive?

I stayed at different places visiting family and friends, and when I was staying with my son, Gordon, and his family, he suggested that I should go with him to his office on the

A Golden Oldie in Cyber Space.

Monday morning before he took me to my mother in Reading as was planned. We had to leave at 6.15 a.m. so that we would beat the mad rush of traffic going into London. By leaving so early, he said we would avoid a whole hour of driving and the frayed nerves that come with sitting in long queues of traffic.

It was dark when we left home and dark when we arrived at his office. The night cleaners were just leaving. There was no one else in the office so he made coffee from the machine, and we chatted. Gordon now had time to explain some of the things I wanted to know about the Internet.

He was a graduate in Technology and was a systems analyst Gradually, staff began to arrive, and Gordon introduced me to members of his team.

"This is my mother, she lives in Australia, is seventy and on the Internet," he said. I staggered at such an introduction. Since when have I been introduced, and my age mentioned? This was something very new to me and I was not sure I liked it.

The young men, dressed in suits looked very smart and handsome. "How are you enjoying your stay in England and what is the weather like now in Australia? Do you like living there?" All questions that needed a reply, and I felt relaxed and happy to chat with these polite young men who seemed interested in what I had to say. Then I suddenly thought, maybe they were being kind to an old lady of seventy. I had never seen myself that way before, but it could be the case. I wondered. Yes, I wondered!

The two months passed so quickly, and soon I was once again back home in Australia. Home with my husband Cy, and

Chang our Chow-Chow. Back to the lovely blue skies and sunshine and back to my computer.

But now there was a difference, for when I send an e-mail to Gordon, I can now visualize his office and see him at his desk. This allows me the opportunity to feel a part of his world and gives me a lot of pleasure. So, Hooray! to Cy, for talking me into going on to the Internet., and for the wonderful world of the computer.

As always, when I had settled back home, I enjoyed reflecting on my holiday and the times I had shared with my family and friends, but stuck in my mind was the way Gordon chose to introduce me to his team. Why did it stay in my in my mind? I know he is a kind young man and would not want to offend me, but I must admit I felt touchy about the fact he had mentioned my age. He had never done that before, so why now, when I was not wanting people to know I was seventy. You get that way when you are older. I was talking about my holiday with a friend, and I happened to mention how I felt about this. She said she completely understood the way my son thought and explained it to me this way.

"Your son was proud of the fact that at your age you have the courage and desire to learn something so very new. He sees you as a 'With it Mum'," she said. "And that is why he chose to introduce you this way". "Really! is that the truth?" I believed my friend and I began to understand what she said and decided she was right!

I realized then that we really are a very special breed us 'Golden Oldies' and we have every reason to be proud of ourselves. Buying a computer takes boldness and courage when you are of an age that has seen a lot of change but knows nothing about this new world of space-age technology. There are words that are used in everyday speech by the younger generation, which we were never taught at school. So that is one disadvantage we start out with, apart from the age factor which reduces our power to retain newly gained knowledge.

However, does it stop us? No! it does not.

We venture forth, confident, stretching our imagination, visiting places never seen before, asking questions and getting answers we don't really comprehend but we read, and we talk to people whilst learning all the time. At the age we are now, our grandparents sat in their rocking chairs, read the daily paper, shuffled about the house never going anywhere or doing much, bent over, worn out and old. Today, we walk tall, watch our health, play tennis, golf, swim, dance, travel and try to have open minds and keep up with the latest happenings in the world.

Yes, I can understand now why my son introduced me to his team of young computer experts by announcing my age and I feel good about it.

I have now installed my Publisher Program all by myself and feel great.

Gordon told me, "Of I course you can do it, Mum, you will find it is easy." He was right, and such faith has to be rewarded, so I had to do it. I also knew Danny would be pleased to see how capable I had become, and he was.

I now self-publish my poetry in books with wonderful designs taken from my software program of 125,000 pictures and have just written a story about my childhood in London during the Blitz and as an Evacuee in Reading. It contains thirteen thousand, five hundred words. I knew how many words there were without having to count them. Just a click with my mouse on *Tools*, then on to *Word Count* and up came 13,500 on my monitor. It was wonderful! I had no idea I had written so much.

Through the Internet, I have had my story accepted by The Imperial War Museum in London. It will go into their Printed Book Section and my poetry will go into their 'Unique Archives of Poetry' of which they are proud (their words). I am now the organizer of a group which gives free performances of Poems, Yarns, and Music. There are fourteen of us and we have a wonderful time together and guess what It is me who designs the flyers we put out and the brochures. My letters are now presented in a professional way with my own design of notepaper and business cards. All made possible with my wonderful computer. Also, I am now able to polish up on my schoolgirl French with the French Program I bought.

There are computer clubs starting for retirees and the clubs are growing in fast numbers with large memberships. As you can see, I still love the gadgets that technology offers me today, and I find I have more fun and interest than I have ever had from any other time saving gadgets I have used in the past except maybe for my sewing machine. I learn more as each day passes and my computer is an important part of my life. I use it every day and love it.

There is so much I want to write, so much to see and so much to learn, it is never ending. It is there at my fingertips, and every penny we have spent on our computer has brought so much into our lives. Having this new world which has opened to us is priceless, especially at our time in life. However, there is a sad part in all of this.

My husband says he has become a Computer Widower. He says this but he doesn't really complain as he says he is very proud of what I do and enjoys the fact that I am at home more these days. The days of being tempted to go out shopping and buy things has gone at last.

However, that beautiful paper with all its different textures and colours I find hard to resist. It really does make the finished work look so much better. I know there is so much new software that I am tempted to buy, but I must look away.

For instance, take the Encyclopaedia Britannica. It is now available on disk. Can you imagine what a difference having that would make? I could get rid of the volumes I have had these past forty years and use the space they take up for something else. That really would be wonderful.

But no! I must resist, I can manage without that, but a Scanner, that is a different thing altogether. That is something I really should have. It would allow me to do so much more, and the prices have come down drastically. So, the brochures say. Of course, there is the latest digital camera. What a wonderful new piece of technology. How wonderful to be able to have one, take photos and put them on to my computer right away. No! No! No! Out of the question! But I can wait, there is plenty of time and I know what I will do. I will ask my three children to give me one as a special present for my Eightieth birthday.

Yes! I think that's what I will do. Just imagine how proud that will make Gordon. He will be able to introduce me then, and say, "This is my Eighty-year-old mother. She lives in Australia, is on the Internet and has a Digital Camera." Great! Yes, I really do like the idea of that!

Now it is 2005 and the world of technology has gone so fast, and my life has changed. Five years ago my husband died and my computer became a true blessing. It allowed me to write and print Cy's epitaph. Writing this, took time and thought and it helped to ease the pain and the loneliness I felt. I was also able to present a booklet to all those present at the Celebration of Cy's Life.

As you can imagine my need to be in touch with my family and friends became essential to my well-being and my computer helped enormously. Life goes on and the age of technology helps in many ways. Hospitals are able to use more equipment to save lives and, in every field, and every day someone benefits from the latest technology.

I had my Scanner, before Cy died and I now have my CD Burner and my Digital Camera. The Encyclopaedia Britannica books have all been given away so I now have the free space I wanted and I have no need for a reference library any more as I just type the name into *Google* and I get everything I need to know. I always thought I was good at spelling. I was when at school. Now to my surprise I find I was not as good as I thought. Luckily my computer can correct misspelled words. This is a great bonus and one I never thought I would have.

Prices have dropped drastically and most people who want one are able to have a computer and some have two or three in their homes now. There are now Laptops, that can play and burn CD's and DVD's.

Burn? Yes, it is called burning when you copy to a disc. The

A Golden Oldie in Cyber Space.

word burning now has a different meaning as do so many other words we used before the new language of computers came into being. After all what did we know as a mouse?

The original mouse and keyboards as we knew them have changed and are now available without leads. The large Monitor screens have been replaced with thin screens that take up less room. Now we have Scanners, Printers, copiers and Fax machines all combined together and the price is very affordable and so it goes on.

Mobile phones now have screens which allows you to see the person you are talking to or to show pictures of where you are, and you can take photos as well.

Digital cameras have come down in price and are being used all the time and photos now are sent direct from one person to another by computer. There is no need to have prints made as we did years ago. So, I get lots of photos from my family and friends in England and from friends all over the world.

The world of technology is growing so fast that it is bewildering, and I love it! I am still interested in the wonders of this Space Age and the new technology that is available but now I must call a halt. But I really would love a flat screen monitor, but do I really need one? Not really!

It is time for me to stop and tell myself 'Enough is Enough!'

"But the years have passed, and it is now 2014. I am eighty-seven and I use my computer every day to stay in touch with my friends and family all over the world. My poetry has been printed as a booklet comprising of eighty poems. I have also written stories and had one article published in the Australian

Women's Weekly. I have my flat screen monitor, my digital camera and am on Skype.

How wise I was when I decided to buy my computer seventeen years ago.

Written by Lorraine Roxon Harrington. Gold Coast, Australia

My Grandson Gabriel 1973-1991

Lorraine Roxon

My world suddenly changed four days ago when I was given the dreadful news that my seventeen-year-old grandson Gabriel was dead.

The shock was so great that I found it impossible to believe at first, but it was true. He was killed in a car crash with three of his friends. One was his girlfriend and all were students at Exeter College. He was not the driver, which gave me some comfort to know that Gabriel was not responsible; a small consolation, but I needed it.

Somehow, finding something positive to cling to in such a tragic situation allowed me to think of other things and I was able to recall the many memories from years ago when Gabriel was a little boy. He was intelligent, cheeky, sometimes rude, a bit precocious maybe but always loveable.

I remember him when he was five and he returned after six months in India and Nepal with his Mum and Dad. They had gone looking for that spiritual world of love and peace. I can hear his little voice now singing

"Hare-krish-in-a, Hare-krish-in-a." That is how he sang it. I expected him to come back with his head shaven but I was happy he still had his long black hair. I remember one time collecting him from his Mum and Dad to spend the weekend with me. He came into my bed in the morning and I said "Shall Nana make us a cup of tea?" And he replied, "No Nana. let's have a chat".

So many thoughts, so many happy memories came flooding back and I saw him as he was then.

In memoriam

I am standing in a beautiful old church in Crediton, Devon, England. Outside the daffodils are just beginning to open their trumpets ready to sing the praises of spring. The sun is shining, but there is no warmth because it is the month of February.

I had left behind the hot sunshine of Australia's Gold Coast to be present at the funeral service of my grandson. I tried not to cry, my son had asked me not to. I had to be brave for my family. I looked around the church. My three-year-old granddaughter Miriam held onto my hand, her mother, my daughter Yolanda, stood silent beside her husband Peter, who was holding their youngest in his arms. Miriam stood still, not a movement, not a sound; so small and yet I knew she understood. She too was being brave.

Three quarters of the church was filled by young people dressed in a style which made them stand out from the other mourners. They wore black, not as a sign of mourning, but because it was their fashion. The girls wore heavy black thick soled boots, thick black stockings, and some had their hair streaked with purple and orange. It saddened me to see these girls spoiling their young bodies with tattoos, which they seemed to display with pride. The boys were dressed in a similar uniform: black jumpers with sleeves so long they covered their hands, holes made deliberately so they could stick their fingers through the cuffs.

These were the children of parents who were in their teens during the sixties, the so-called Baby Boomers. Once more I witnessed the cries of protest I had heard in the sixties. The youth of today were trying to say something; trying to be heard and hoping the older generation would listen. The message was the same as it always has been: the eternal voice of youth crying out for justice and equality. I knew that there was no one out there listening. This is the new generation, 'new- age travellers' they call themselves now, and many are just like their parents when they were young, full of energy, hope, passion and ideals.

They, too, believe they can change the world and make it a better place for everyone and so they should think this way; for it is only while they are young that they will be able to experience such strong emotions and believe with so much conviction.

We of the older generation know that message. We spouted it

in the forties and our parents did the same in the thirties and their parents did the same after World War One.

Sadly it is always the same message; the only difference is the uniform we choose to wear. Today long hair is not so acceptable.

The Beatles era is a long way away. I noticed some of the boys had shaved heads, even some of the girls. Body piercing was the latest look and earrings were shown in abundance on areas never used in my day. For the older generation this was far from adding to their beauty but the purpose was to be noticed and stand out from the crowd. You could almost hear them saying, "Look at us, we are different. Take note of us and what we are saying; listen to us before it is too late."

I looked around the church and was suddenly aware of their grief and in that moment I knew these were my grandson's friends and I suddenly felt that I knew him better. Seeing his friends grieving, I could sense that he was loved by them and was able to feel sad for them and I realised then that whatever differences there were in our ages, our dress, the way we think, and our beliefs, we all share grief in the same way when tragedy hits us. We all cry, but sadly our crying can never be equal to the tears shed by the parents of a dead child.

My thoughts turned to Gabriel's brother Owen and I wondered how he would cope without his older sibling. I looked at him and saw that he too was trying to be brave. Maybe my son had also told him not to cry.

A young man played a guitar and a girl sang. I imagined they were songs that Gabriel liked and I was surprised that amongst them was a Beatles song. It brought back many memories and I looked back to the days when our home was full with the constant sound of their music. I loved the music of the Beatles and still do, even though their music brings back memories that are not so pleasant to remember. It also brings back memories of how I had once dreaded that I might stand, as I do now, but mourning the loss of my eldest son Manfred, Gabriel's father.

As I look at my grandson's coffin, I give thanks for having been spared such a tragedy and I imagine the dreadful suffering my son and his wife are going through. Life would never be the same again for them, and I could hold back my tears no longer.

I cried for them, I cried for myself and for all of us, and how all our lives would be changed forever. I cried for my grandson Gabriel and in my crying I mourned the fact that I had not known him better.

I left England when Gabriel was six years old, returning every few years to visit the family. I was there to share his eleventh birthday and last year when he was seventeen. He had grown to be a tall, handsome young man, showing signs of a highly intelligent mind. When he was sixteen I had letters telling me that he had started a crèche for the students' children, and was Vice President of the Students Union.

The letters were not from Gabriel, I never expected him to write. Grandchildren hardly ever write to grandparents these days. I was proud of him and his ideals. For one so young he had a conscience and was trying to make the world a better place just as his mother and his father had tried to in the sixties when they believed 'All you need is love'.

I had made so many plans for the day when Gabriel would visit me and I would show him our beautiful Australian beaches, the lush green hinterland, and our great rain forests. He would know the heat of the Australian sun and I would enjoy watching him swim and surf. This would be our time to get to know each other as friends and share our thoughts and talk as adults. These were my hopes and dreams. Now, suddenly they had all been taken away.

The last time I saw Gabriel was a year ago when he waved me off at Exeter railway station. At the time I looked at him and felt sad that he was so scruffy. His jumper was new but he had torn it deliberately to put his fingers through a cuff-hole he had made. His track shoes were in ribbons and dirty.

My daughter-in-law Liz was complaining; she was embarrassed and I knew how she felt. I had felt the same years ago when Manfred had got on the bus with me with his long hair, band around his forehead and tatty Afghan coat and sandals on a cold winters day. Knowing I would be ashamed for people to know that he was with me, he deliberately said in a loud voice, "Hello Mum", and took the seat beside me. I remember laughing and feeling pleased that he was there. I was starting to realise then that what he wore and the way he looked were unimportant. He was here beside me; he was alive.

I told Liz to accept Gabriel as he was, even though it may be difficult. I was able to give such advice because I knew that one day he would marry and have children, just as his father and mother had. I knew that when that happens most of us are too busy coping with our everyday existence and are left with little time to follow our ideals and dreams. After all, it happens to most of us, doesn't it? I know it did with me and my parents.

I looked at the sun shining through the stained glass windows of the church and once more my thoughts returned to that day when I last saw Gabriel and I longed so much for him to be here, scruffy and wearing his torn jumper. But instead he was in this lovely old church, lying in a coffin, gone from us forever.

I try to tell myself that maybe he is in a better place, where the injustices of life do not exist. Maybe he has been spared seeing his passion for justice and equality slowly silenced by the everyday act of living. Maybe he will be spared hearing those once so strong youthful voices, gradually become the feeble voices of the old asking, "Where did all our dreams go? What happened to all our hopes and plans for a better future? How could such a passionate need for justice die? And where did all the loving go?"

I would like to think my grandson will return one day when the world is a better place, when there is peace and tolerance towards all people and there is justice. This is my hope. Call it rationalisation, call it what you will, all I know is I cannot believe Gabriel has gone forever.

Three years after his passing the College named the crèche after Gabriel which was a much appreciated gesture by all those who loved him.

Written 1992. By Lorraine Roxon. Edited by Miriam Bentham November 2014.

We Are What We Are

Lorraine Harrington

My husband was a psychiatrist and it was the practice at the time for the mental hospitals to offer rental houses for their doctors, their families and some members of staff. As the hospitals were situated five miles away from the nearest town it was important that doctors were on hand. They were large Victorian mansions usually situated away from the town centre.

We rented one of the houses which was situated in the sprawling hospital grounds. The hospital was called 'The Pastures' and it was in Mickleover, Derby, England. We had two children, Manfred who was seven and Yolanda who was four.

This was in the late fifties and was at the time when mental hospitals were enormous. These large hospitals were known as mental asylums and were established to care for the mentally sick who needed to be looked after in secure, secluded premises either for their own good or for the good of the local community.

Years ago a young unmarried girl could be classed as being of unsound mind because she was young, sexually active and pregnant. Very often the family agreed for their daughter to be admitted in order to save the disgrace this could bring to them. Many of these wrongly diagnosed people grew old and became institutionalised by hospital life. Sadly after years of living in this enclosed and protected atmosphere they were incapable of functioning in the world outside and so they were looked after with food, poor clothing and accommodation.

Some women who were considered capable worked under supervision as domestics in the hospital. Also under supervision some men worked as labourers and farm hands. The hospitals had farms and beautiful gardens and allotments where they grew vegetables for the hospital use.

In the 50's and 60's many changes started to take place in the Mental Health system. This was brought about by the drug companies and the new medications they were discovering which allowed mentally ill patients to be treated successfully. Many patients on the new drugs were found to be capable to go outside the hospital grounds and to the town to shop but always under supervision.

In light of the new changes that were happening, the Mental Health authorities decided patients who worked, should receive some form of pocket money for their labour. A few of the female patients who were already working in the wards as domestics were offered work in the homes of the doctors who lived in the grounds.

This was all part of the new rehabilitation scheme for the mentally ill which was slowly coming into force.

I had a female patient, Celia, who helped in the house but was never left alone.

The wives and children of doctors living in the grounds shared a bond as we were all young families and the husbands were all studying with the aim to reach the top of their profession and become consultants.

Hugo was one of these doctors and Jean, his wife and I developed a good friendship. Jean had three boys: Norman, who was four and twin boys, John and Scott who were just over a year old.

They were so good and well behaved and Jean was the perfect wife and mother. She was the epitome of what I wanted to be. Her home was always tidy with everything in its place.

She even had *Royal Doulton* Figurines on a low shelf which could have easily been damaged by little children. I would never have taken the chance but Jean's boys did as they were told and Jean had told them not to touch.

The fact that she had been a theatre Sister convinced me that was the reason why she ran her home in such an orderly fashion. I wanted so much to be organised like Jean. When she invited me for coffee, she wrote the time and my name on a board in her kitchen. I remember jokingly saying to her. "Do you need to write down when I am coming to you? Surely having me for coffee is something you would look forward to and would not likely forget?" I liked to tease her!

I can see the scene so well after all these years. Going to have coffee at Jean's in the morning meant the house smelt of lunch cooking. The twins would already be upstairs, lying quietly in their cots having their regular morning nap. There would be a tray laid with two cups and saucers and a plate of homemade biscuits.

The aroma of coffee would greet me and Jean would be dressed, relaxed and sitting with a cigarette in her hand waiting for me. How wonderful she was! I had left my house with loads of ironing waiting to be done, beds unmade and the breakfast dishes waiting to be washed.

It was not the way I wanted to be, but there you are, that was me. But if only I could be like Jean! As time went by our friendship grew stronger. We took turns collecting the children from school and looked after each other's children when one of us needed to go to the local shops. I was auntie to her three boys and she was auntie to my son and daughter.

Later Jean had the little girl she wanted so much and I had another much wanted son. Before my youngest was born my husband got a position as a consultant psychiatrist in Yorkshire.

Doctors had to climb the ladder taking on a higher position in their field in order to reach the height of their profession and this meant moving each time when another post was taken. This was an accepted fact and most wives were prepared for this and moved house each time uprooting their children and leaving their friends. So it was with a heavy heart, and with a new baby we left Derby and moved to Yorkshire. It was much harder this time as the children were older and leaving their friends. Having to go to a new school was not easy for them.

The hospital in Yorkshire was just like 'The Pastures', the one we had left in Derby. Miles away from the nearest town surrounded by acres of grounds and with the land farmed and the grounds kept beautifully by the male patients with orderlies overseeing them. Over the years I had got used to seeing patients walking around the grounds and some would look at my babies when they were in their prams and talk to them as if they knew them.

It was sad to see some of the women call them by a certain name as if they thought it was a child they knew.

So again we lived in a rented house in the hospital grounds just as we did in Derby but this house was much older and the children had to go a long way to school. It was not a village school that my children had been used to and the change was dramatic for them. We all had to make new friends, and I missed the friends I had in Derby.

With a new baby taking up so much of my time and with no Celia to help, the children became difficult and were unhappy. So it was not a good time for the family.

During these years we had rented out our house in London but now my husband had reached the position he had worked for all these years it was time to settle down. Manfred was now eleven and about to take his eleven plus exam and I felt it was time for the children to have a more stable school life. So we sold the London house and moved away from the hospital.

We bought a rambling Victorian family house with an orchard, large lawns and fields around us in a lovely country village called Honley near Holmfirth, of popular TV sitcom fame, *Last of the Summer Wine*.

I wanted to make a new start and although I was a good cook, sewed clothes for myself and my children, always had dinner on time and my children were never late for school it was never good enough for me. It was not like the way Jean organised her home life.

In my eyes Jean was the epitome of everything I wanted to be.

Just about this time, Jean's husband also received a post as a Consultant in a Yorkshire Hospital which was about twenty five miles away from where we were now living.

I missed Jean and it was wonderful when she moved nearer to us. Almost two years had passed and in that time we had been back to Derby and spent a few days with Hugo and Jean but now we were able to be in contact more often and that was good.

One morning when the children had left for school and my husband had gone to the hospital, I phoned Jean. With the new home I had decided it was my chance to make a change. I was going to be like Jean from now on and most of all I wanted Jean to know. So I phoned her.

"Do you know Jean, I feel so good. We have just finished breakfast and I have washed all the dishes and put them away. The children have just caught their bus for school and I am dressed in a navy blue button through overall, instead of being in my nightie and dressing gown and my long hair is already combed and in a bun."

I was sure Jean would be impressed.

I decided I would not mention the fact that a big lump of clay I was sculpting was lying on the top of my washing machine and the beds had not yet been made.

The phone suddenly went quiet. I thought we had been cut off as there was no sound, but then Jean spoke.

"Now!" she said, "I have something to tell you! Why do you want to be like me? I have always admired the way you live your life.

"I loved the smell of the bread you used to make, the lovely cakes and the sewing you did and the laid back easy way you lived. The way you came back from shopping and always had to rummage to the bottom of your bag for goodies you had bought for the children. I can see you now! The children all eager and you pulling out all sorts of things till you got to the bottom of the bag to find their treats. It was a ritual we expected and one we would not have wanted to change. Nothing seemed too much bother for you and you always had time for people. You never made an issue of anything and always seemed to glide through difficulties with an ease which I never could muster. Even if you were busy and no matter what mess you were in, you always stopped, sat down, made a cup of tea and made a friend feel they were welcome.

"As for me? Well... I have to know what is happening. I have to plan in advance so everything is in order. I dust and clean, I cook and wash even though I have help in the home. I have to have everything just so! I cannot leave dishes after a meal and sit and have a cigarette like you do. I make the beds and turn back the covers so they are ready to climb into. I know I get cross if the children don't put things away after they use them. I now suffer with high blood pressure and the children have lovingly given me the nickname 'Mrs Homecare' because I have every kitchen gadget they sell. My doctor has told me I have to take things easy and I have to change the way I live.

"So now you will be surprised by what I am going to tell you.

"As we speak, I am in my dressing gown and nightie and have just seen the children off to school and couldn't care less who has seen me like this. The dirty breakfast dishes are still on the table and I feel relaxed, comfortable and happy. I am sitting having a cup of coffee and a cigarette. Now what do you think about that?"

I was astounded! I was lost for words. I could not believe what Jean had just told me. Be like me? So disorganised. "I don't think that's a good idea Jean, that's just not you!"

"Don't say that! This is me! This is the me I want to be. This is the me I need to be," she said. I could not believe it. How could my perfect friend possibly want to be like me?

We chatted on about all sorts of things as we always did and when I finally rang off, I felt stunned. I sat down in my tidy kitchen, took off the button through overall which was hot and uncomfortable, made a cup of tea, lit a cigarette and thought about Jean and what she had said.

It was all wrong! Jean could not be like me. She never could. It would be impossible. Half an hour went by and I sat and thought and had another cigarette. Then something special happened to me. It suddenly dawned on me. Jean had no choice but to be the way she was. It was no good her trying to be like me and no good my trying to be like her.

We are what we are!

I liked her for the way she was and she liked me for the way I was. So why did we want to change?

That day I decided that I would forget about trying to be like Jean and I would go back to the way I was and the way my family knew me. I never wanted my life to be tied to a timetable routine as Jean's was.

That was nearly forty years ago and what I learned that day has stayed with me. I found just being me was hard enough without trying to be someone else.

Lorraine Roxon Harrington. September 2003.

It is now 2012. Jean has passed away and sadly the last eight years of her life she had to be cared for as she had a stroke. I lived in Australia but kept in touch. I would phone her and she would pick up the phone and then leave it without talking. Her son John, one of the twins, who I have known for fifty years, helped me by taking his mobile phone to Jean so we could have a short chat. John is a very kind man and has a wife and two daughters and after all these years he still sees me as his auntie and is in contact with me.

I write poetry and this is a poem I wrote for Jean:

For Jean

2nd March 2009

I admired the way Jean managed her life
A good mother, a friend, a companion, a wife.
Her home always tidy, no dust to be seen
Always calm and collected was my friend Jean.
The washing and ironing all put away
The twins in their cots, Norman out to play
Her work was all done her time to relax
A coffee, a cigarette, phone a friend, have a chat
I so much wanted to be like Jean
To be organised, tidy and looking serene
But strange as it sounds and it's hard to believe
Jean told me she wanted to be like me.
I suppose with my gregarious ways
No plans, no routine, just live for today
Might have seemed attractive to someone like Jean
Who was always so organised tidy and clean
Though we have lived many miles apart
The bond that we shared was made to last
She has left this world but is still with me
My wonderful dearest and loving friend, Jean

Jennifer's Ride

Lorraine Roxon

Jennifer has spina bifida and is the daughter of my friend Thelma. When she was a little girl she could walk with callipers but now she is thirty two and is in a wheelchair.

She has an infection which is causing her a lot of problems and she has recently been given the sad news that the specialists are considering a full hind quarter amputation on her.

Jennifer has been confined to a wheelchair for quite a few years now, but she manages to look after herself and is a very lively, intelligent and cheerful single young woman with a family and friends who love and care about her.

Jennifer had an appointment to see the specialist and as usual Thelma took her. Jennifer lives in Ipswich and it is a long drive from the Gold Coast so I went with Thelma to keep her company. I was there with them at the hospital when they received the devastating news about a possible amputation.

We all left the Hospital in Brisbane feeling very low and found it hard to talk or even try to make conversation. Because it had been a tiring day and because Thelma understandably wanted to have more time with Jennifer we stayed the night. I found it hard to sleep, thinking about Jennifer and the prognosis she had received that day.

To do something that would make her feel happy was foremost in my mind and I thought about the wonderful group of people I knew who belonged to the Motor Cycle club. If only I could get her a ride on a motorbike I knew she would be thrilled especially as Jennifer had experienced a Harley ride once before. It had been a special treat for her twenty-first birthday; the family had paid and she loved it.

I phoned my friend Frank Murray who rode with a group of motor bikers. He kindly suggested that I should contact Kevin and Morag, who happened to live in Ipswich.

"They are a lovely couple and I am sure they will be happy to help," Frank said. And so when I got back home, I rang Morag and Kevin who, as Frank had said, were wonderful. They said they would be only too happy to take Jennifer for a ride.

So it was arranged that Thelma and I would go to Jennifer's and we would all meet at Kevin and Morag's in two weeks time at 10.a.m on the Sunday. I had specially charged my video camera so that there would be a complete record of this special day; I began filming as Jennifer rang the doorbell and continued till the journey ended.

Jennifer's Ride

It was wonderful to see the caring way Kevin and Morag helped Jennifer to sit comfortably on the back of Kevin's beautiful shiny bike.

We had expected to ride for half an hour and were surprised when Kevin announced the ride would be to Toowoomba which was an hour's journey. We were thrilled but wondered if Jennifer would be able to stay on the bike for so long. It would be quite a long ride!

Thelma and I would be in the car following, with Jennifer's wheel chair in the boot should she need to stop. With Jennifer sitting upright on the back of Kevin's bike with a beaming smile on her face with helmet, leather jacket and gloves, all supplied by Morag and Kevin we finally took off. Riding behind Morag on her bike and Kevin on his and with Jennifer sitting upright and with the sun shining on the beautiful countryside it was the start to a perfect day and we were very happy.

We finally arrived at Toowoomba and drove up to a cafe where Jennifer had a Subway which she loved while we had a coffee and sandwich. Jennifer had no problem with the long drive and when we got back, Morag and Kevin kindly invited us in for tea so we could watch the video on their big screen.

With many words of gratitude, lots of hugs and promises that Jennifer would be invited over for a barbecue one day, we finally left Morag and Kevin.

Thelma had driven a lot and was tired; we were keen to see the film again and talk about the wonderful time we all had so we ended up staying the night. Unlike my last stay, this time I was able to sleep well and it was all due to Frank Murray for his helpful suggestion and for the kindness of Kevin and Morag who gave a young woman with spina bifida, a wonderful day to remember.

The best part of the story is that Jennifer never had the operation we all feared. She met and married David two years later. I was asked to write a poem and read it at their wedding.
(Story written by Lorraine Roxon Harrington. Edited by Yolanda Bentham)

Jennifer and David September 2nd 2006

Today we have witnessed a wedding
The joining of two people in love
Vows have been made before us all
With blessings from up above.
Marriage is not always easy
It needs commitment to survive
Lots of love, respect and laughter
Helps a marriage stay alive.
Jenny and David have been together
Have had time to find the key
That opens the door to happiness
And lets love shine from within.
Knowing this couple as we do
We are certain their future will flourish
For they possess those essential qualities
Of loyalty of love and of courage.
Commitment has now been taken
Together they start a new life
David is Jennifer's husband
And Jennifer is now David's wife.
We give our love to both of them
And we could talk about them all day
But we will leave it to their families
Who will say all we want to say.

www.ingramcontent.com/pod-product-compliance
Lightning Source LLC
LaVergne TN
LVHW032012070526
838202LV00059B/6416